T0144715

Sacred Fire

THE QBR 100
ESSENTIAL BLACK BOOKS

MAX RODRIGUEZ, Founder, *QBR: The Black Review*
ANGELI R. RASBURY
CAROL TAYLOR

Foreword by CHARLES JOHNSON

John Wiley & Sons, Inc.
New York • Chichester • Weinheim • Brisbane • Singapore • Toronto

Copyright © 1999 by Max Rodriguez and Angeli R. Rasbury. All rights reserved.
Published by John Wiley & Sons, Inc.
Published simultaneously in Canada

Library of Congress Cataloging-in-Publication Data:

Sacred fire : the QBR 100 essential black books / [compiled and edited by] Max Rodriguez, Angeli R. Rasbury, Carol Taylor; foreword by Charles Johnson.
    p. cm.
    Includes bibliographical references (p.   ) and index.
    ISBN: 978-1-620-45787-0
    1. Afro-Americans—Books and reading.   I. Rodriguez, Max.
II. Rasbury, Angeli R.   III. Taylor, Carol.
Z1361.N39S22   1999
[E185]
016.973'0496073—dc21   98-35060

10 9 8 7 6 5 4 3 2 1

Sacred Fire

To my father, who kept his eyes on the prize;
my mother, who introduced me to Bach, Billie, and Bustelo;
and my brother, who found his own way.

—Max Rodriguez

For my nieces and nephews, who already show
a love for black books.

—Didi

O Black and Unknown Bards of long ago,
How came your lips to touch the sacred fire?

—James Weldon Johnson
"O Black and Unknown Bards"

Contents

Acknowledgments   xv

Foreword by Charles Johnson   xvii

Introduction   1

Origins, Ancestors, and Memory

Commentary by Charles Brooks   9

*The Interesting Narrative of the Life of Olaudah Equiano,
or Gustavus Vassa, the African, Written by Himself*
by Olaudah Equiano   13

*The Narrative of the Life and Times of Frederick Douglass:
An American Slave, Written by Himself* by Frederick
Douglass   15

*Clotel: or, the President's Daughter, A Narrative of Slave
Life in the United States* by William Wells Brown   17

*Our Nig, or Sketches from the Life of a Free Black, in a
Two-Story White House, North* by Harriet E. Wilson   19

Up from Slavery by Booker T. Washington   22

Black Reconstruction in America by W. E. B. Du Bois   24

From Slavery to Freedom: A History of African Americans
by John Hope Franklin   26

Stolen Legacy by George G. M. James   28

Before the Mayflower by Lerone Bennett Jr.   30

Two Thousand Seasons by Ayi Kwei Armah   32

They Came Before Columbus by Ivan Van Sertima   33

Roots: The Saga of an American Family by Alex Haley   35

Sally Hemings by Barbara Chase-Riboud   37

The Chaneysville Incident by David Bradley   38

Beloved by Toni Morrison   40

Kindred by Octavia Butler   43

*Spirits of the Passage: The Transatlantic Slave Trade in
    the Seventeenth Century* by Madeline Burnside and
    Rosemarie Robotham   45

Community and Identity

Commentary by Robert Fleming   49

Lyrics of Lowly Life by Paul Laurence Dunbar   53

The Conjure Woman by Charles Chestnutt   55

The Souls of Black Folk by W. E. B. Du Bois   56

Cane by Jean Toomer   58

The New Negro by Alain Locke   59

The Blacker the Berry by Wallace Thurman   61

The Mis-education of the Negro by Carter G. Woodson   62

The Ways of White Folks by Langston Hughes   64

Black Boy by Richard Wright   66

*Black Metropolis: A Study of Negro Life in a Northern
    City* by St. Clair Drake and Horace R. Cayton   68

Invisible Man by Ralph Ellison   70

Go Tell It on the Mountain by James Baldwin   72

Things Fall Apart by Chinua Achebe   74

A Raisin in the Sun by Lorraine Hansberry   76

Blues People: Negro Music in White America by LeRoi Jones   78

Jubilee by Margaret Walker   80

Black Skin, White Masks by Frantz Fanon   82

The Crisis of the Negro Intellectual by Harold Cruse   84

We a BaddDDD People by Sonia Sanchez   86

The Hero and the Blues by Albert Murray   87

Song of Solomon by Toni Morrison   88

Elbow Room by James Alan McPherson   90

Damballah by John Edgar Wideman   91

*A Hard Road to Glory: A History of the African
    American Athlete* by Arthur Ashe   93

Krik? Krak! by Edwidge Danticat   95

Politics, Nationalism, and Revolution

Commentary by Arthur Flowers   99

David Walker's Appeal by David Walker   103

*The Philosophy and Opinions of Marcus Garvey;
    or Africa for the Africans* by Marcus Garvey   105

Black Bourgeoisie by E. Franklin Frazier   107

The Fire Next Time by James Baldwin   109

The Black Jacobins by C. L. R. James   111

The Wretched of the Earth by Frantz Fanon   112

Africa Must Unite by Dr. Kwame Nkrumah   113

The River Between by Ngugi Wa Thiongo   115

Black Power by Stokely Carmichael and Charles V.
    Hamilton   116

Soul on Ice by Eldridge Cleaver   118

Soledad Brother: The Prison Letters of George Jackson
    by George Jackson   119

Seize the Time: The Story of the Black Panther Party
    by Bobby Seale   121

The Destruction of Black Civilization by Chancellor
    Williams   123

The Spook Who Sat by the Door by Sam Greenlee   125

Notes of a Hanging Judge by Stanley Crouch   127

Race Matters by Cornel West   129

God's Bits of Wood by Sembene Ousmane   131

Soul and Spirit

Commentary by Hazel Reid   135

Jesus and the Disinherited by Howard Thurman   139

Letter from a Birmingham Jail by Martin Luther King Jr.   141

A Black Theology of Liberation by James H. Cone   143

Mumbo Jumbo by Ishmael Reed   145

Faith and the Good Thing by Charles Johnson   146

The Famished Road by Ben Okri   147

Tapping the Power Within by Iyanla Vanzant   149

*Conversations with God: Two Centuries of Prayers
    by African Americans* by James Melvin Washington   151

*Guide My Feet: Prayers and Meditation on Loving and
    Working for Children* by Marian Wright Edelman   153

*My Soul Is a Witness: African American Women's
    Spirituality,* edited by Gloria Wade-Gayles   155

*The Substance of Things Hoped For: A Memoir of
    African American Faith* by Samuel DeWitt Proctor   157

Sisters' Stories

Commentary by Eisa Nefetari Ulen   161

Their Eyes Were Watching God by Zora Neale Hurston   165

The Street by Ann Petry   167

Annie Allen by Gwendolyn Brooks   168

Maud Martha by Gwendolyn Brooks   170

I Know Why the Caged Bird Sings by Maya Angelou   171

The Autobiography of Miss Jane Pittman by Ernest Gaines   174

for colored girls who have considered suicide/when the
    rainbow is enuf by Ntozake Shange   176

Black Macho and the Myth of the Superwoman
    by Michele Wallace   178

The Women of Brewster Place by Gloria Naylor   179

The Color Purple by Alice Walker   180

Praisesong for the Widow by Paule Marshall   183

Sister Outsider: Essays and Speeches by Audre Lorde   185

Waiting to Exhale by Terry McMillan   187

Your Blues Ain't Like Mine by Bebe Moore Campbell   188

Kehinde by Buchi Emecheta   189

The Daughters of Africa, edited by Margaret Busby   190

Sojourner Truth: A Life, a Symbol by Nell Irvin Painter   192

Brothers' Lives

Commentary by S. E. Anderson   197

Native Son by Richard Wright   201

If He Hollers Let Him Go by Chester Himes   202

The Autobiography of Malcolm X as told to Alex Haley   204

Manchild in the Promised Land by Claude Brown   206

Brothers and Keepers by John Edgar Wideman   207

Fences by August Wilson   208

The Man Who Cried I Am by John Alfred Williams   209

The Life of Langston Hughes by Arnold Rampersad   210

Miles: The Autobiography by Miles Davis and
    Quincy Troupe   212

A Lesson Before Dying by Ernest Gaines   214

W. E. B. Du Bois: Biography of a Race by David
    Levering Lewis   215

Black Betty by Walter Mosley   216

Brotherman, edited by Herb Boyd and Robert Allen   218

Index of Books by Title   219

Index of Books by Author   223

Index of Books by Genre   226

Acknowledgments

The editors would like to thank the following for their generous assistance in the compilation of our list of 100 great books: Malaika Adero, Molefi Kete Asante, William M. Banks, Amiri Baraka, Betty Winston Bayé, Herb Boyd, Ed and Miriam Carter, James Fugate, Archie Givens, Suheir Hammad, Charles Johnson, Rosalind Oliphant Jones, Jacqueline C. Jones, Ph.D., Andre Kelton, Paul E. Logan, Zakiyya McCloud, Sonia Sanchez, Anne Allen Shockley, the staff of Afrikan World Books, the staff of Brother's Books, the staff of Nkiru Books, the staff of Sisterspace and Books. We would also like to thank the many supporters of QBR who recommended books, including Reinaldo Cummings, Jr., Dorothea Moore, Loretta J. Hargrove, Sandra D. Cahse, Rita Woods, and Margarita Smith-Phillips.

Max Rodriguez would like to honor those who have come before us, whose struggle has garnered for us life and the begrudging respect of survival. He offers love and gratitude to his wife, Melba, without whom QBR could not have been sustained. He offers gratitude to Jeri Love-Graves and Patrick Lee, the original QBR team; to every QBR contributor and writer; to supporters and volunteers who, through QBR, have expressed their love of books and black people—what a combination; to QBR editors Tonya Bolden, Susan McHenry, and Leslie Lockhart; to the writers and recorders of revolution and accommodation: Haki Madhubuti, Sonia Sanchez, Paul Coates, Glenn Thompson, Kassahun Checole; to the QBR advisory board, who gave me hell *and* tremendous support; to Chris Jackson, my editor at Wiley, an astounding individual as deep in his knowledge of African American literature as patience. He drove me firmly but gently, and always with good direction. Finally (and first), I offer a deep and reverent gratitude to the All for being allowed. Thank you.

Angeli R. Rasbury would also like to thank Shanida Smith, Monique Fleming Berg, and her family for being so patient with her and supportive.

Foreword

by Charles Johnson

As we approach a new century, it is difficult to resist the temptation of composing briefs for the best artistic products—novels, poetry, plays, and motion pictures—of the last hundred years, though clearly such selection by its very nature must be provisional and woefully incomplete. Often they become lightning rods for controversy, because at century's end we are still immersed in what many call the Culture Wars. Consider the literary world's flap over the haphazardly selected "100 Best English-Language Novels" compiled by the editorial board of the Modern Library, a canon that included only three black books (*Native Son, Invisible Man,* and *Go Tell It on the Mountain*), all of them unquestionably superior and seminal works of art, but written exclusively by males and published before 1955 or, put another way, prior to the civil rights and Black Power movements. It was a statement saying, in effect, that the last half-century of black literary production is unworthy of notice, or that the jury is still out on the enduring value of these texts. Fortunately, this Waspish catalogue soon lost all credibility and was judged capricious once the bungling selection process was revealed (one editorial board member confessed to recommending books he had not read), just as a giggle factor now clings to the "100 Top American Films" announced by the American Film Institute. That much-publicized list included not a single motion picture written, directed, or produced by persons of color. (What? No Charles Burnett? No Oscar Micheaux?)

Thus, Max Rodriguez, publisher of QBR and author of the book in your hands, is dead-on right when he says in his introduction that black Americans still live "within a society that has institutionalized its efforts to relegate blackness to the bottom

xvii

rung." This book you hold, this "view of the African American literary mind, circa 1999," is a necessary antidote to the nervous tokenism of the Modern Library list, to the aesthetic apartheid practiced by the American Film Institute, and to this culture's intractable resistance to recognizing the contributions of the African Diaspora. But readers *will* ask, and so must I, the inevitable question: Is QBR's inventory of literary excellence complete, coherent, and consistent?

If I were to sift through black writing in *one* genre only (novels, say), looking for literary gold, my criterion would be identical to and not differ one iota from that of Albert Murray, who wisely informed us in *The Blue Devils of Nada* that fine art is distinguished by its "range, precision, profundity, and the idiomatic subtlety of the rendition." With Murray as my guide, I would hunt for books that exhibited and promoted in their readers a refinement of language, perception, and reflection. The majority of authors cited here do just that; they are watershed thinkers like the polyhistor W. E. B. Du Bois, magisterial storytellers like Ralph Ellison, and writers whose works—from slave narratives to contemporary cultural critiques—have proven to be essential for a firm grasp of both black and American history.

Yet, no list of 100 will please everyone, and some readers will kvetch about the omissions, fine writers, and first-rate, elegant minds who somehow fell through the cracks: groundbreaking science fiction writer Samuel Delany; Pulitzer Prize–winning Poet Laureate Rita Dove; Clarence Major, our magister ludi of literary experimentation; essayist Gerald Early, a craftsman who writes with clarity and astonishing precision; the late Leon Forrest; MacArthur poet Jay Wright; the ubiquitous black intellectuals— the prolific Thomas Sowell from the right and Henry Louis Gates from the left.

I could go on, of course. Whenever we choose to tally books for a new "canon" of black writing, there will be objections, counter-lists, and fungible choices. More important, though, the very enterprise of making a checklist compels us all, as readers, to question the presuppositions and values we bring to literary judgments. It forces us, if nothing else, to define our own aesthetic position. Is a work "essential" because it was a bestseller? (In that case Stephen King and Irving Wallace are essential.) Because it is "political"—i.e., one that jibes with our own political views? Or won a prestigious award? Or do we gravitate toward certain authors because they are celebrities and appear charming, witty, and well dressed under the klieg lights on *The Oprah Winfrey Show*? Needless to say, none of this has much of anything to do with literary and intellectual achievement, though it does reveal the merely commercial or marketing aspects of contemporary publishing, where too often books are just commodities to be sold—as we sell burritos and toilet paper—and authors are not bellwethers for the life of the mind, but salespersons primarily concerned with profits and the bottom line.

So yes, every list raises interesting questions. Yet what was said in defense of the Modern Library canon—that it briefly galvanized street sales and got more people reading its number one choice, James Joyce's *Ulysses*—can be said as well for the QBR inventory. If it encourages black people to read, it also serves the goal of achieving black *freedom*. No, I do not mean this merely in a "political" way (though surely reading these texts serves this end), but rather in the deepest philosophical sense. Look around you. What do you see? We are enveloped, I daresay, by what Saul Bellow in his essay "Culture Now" called "an amusement society, like decadent Rome." Many Americans watch eight hours of television daily—ready-made images they *passively* receive, even as they consume the endless, often vulgar products of a Hollywood that targets adolescents as its primary audience. In the midst of formulaic entertainment, in a popular culture where "dumbing down" is the rule, *reading* becomes the most radical of all enterprises.

Open any novel. What is there? Black marks—signs—on white paper. First they are silent. They are lifeless, lacking signification until the consciousness of the reader imbues them with meaning, allowing a fictitious character like Bigger Thomas, say, to emerge hugely from the monotonous rows of ebony type. Once this magical act takes place in the mind of the reader, an entire fictional world appears, redivivus, in his consciousness: "a vivid and continuous dream," as novelist John Gardner once called it, one that so ensorcells us that we forget the room we're sitting in or fail to hear the telephone ring. Put simply, the world experienced within any book is *transcendent*. It exists for consciousness alone (Bigger exists *only* as a mental construct, like a mathematical entity). But, as Jean-Paul Sartre describes so well in his classic work, *What Is Literature?*, the rare experience found in books is the "conjoint effort of author and reader." It is dialectical. While the writer composes his "world" in words, his (or her) work requires an attentive reader who will "put himself from the very beginning and almost without a guide at the height of this silence" of signs. Reading, Sartre tells us, is *directed creation*. A contract of sorts. "To write is to make an appeal to the reader that he lead into objective existence the revelation which I have undertaken by means of language." Do you get it? I hope so. For each book *requires* that a reader exercise his orbific freedom for the "world" and theater of meaning embodied on its pages to *be*. As readers, we invest the cold signs on the pages of *Native Son* with our *own* emotions, *our* understanding of poverty, oppression, and fear; then, in what is almost an act of thaumaturgy, the powerful figures and tropes Wright has created reward us richly by returning our subjective feelings to us transformed, refined, and alchemized by language into a new vision with the capacity to change our lives forever.

This magic rests in your hands, as readers. It is a power to co-create and travel through numerous imaginative and intellectual realms that you can invoke at any time, anywhere. If film is a communal experience, as so many have claimed, then reading is the triumph of individual consciousness and man's freedom. And, despite the issues raised by any list of "essential" books, QBR's evolving canon is a splendid way to begin flexing the muscles of our minds and honoring black literary artists by allowing their too often marginalized contributions to find a place to permanently live within us.

Seattle, Washington
1998

Introduction

QBR: The Black Book Review was established five years ago to provide a forum for the critical review and celebration of books that captured our voices, our stories, and our lives. We've taken it as our responsibility and mission to praise and admonish our writers, as needed, and to expose their work to our readers in an unprecedented way.

This book is an outgrowth of that mission. While we have traditionally exposed our readers to the work of our best contemporary writers, for the purposes of this book, it was our intent to gather a consensus on the literature that has most impacted us as a community across the years. Not just the latest flowering of critically and commercially successful literature (although it's good that we continue to develop as a market), but the classics: the works that represent the record of our collective experience. We wanted to find out how important the written history of our experience is to us today. So we asked.

Our request was very simple and straightforward: Name ten books by authors from the African Diaspora that have had the greatest impact on you. We asked everyone. (I know, I know, but we *almost* asked you.) We asked scholars and historians (they read, too); bookstore owners and book buyers; members of reading clubs and attendees at QBR's literary series. (I even asked my sister.) We drew from this survey a range of books that identified the issues and philosophies that we, as a people, felt were most critical, and that were written by the artists who most eloquently and powerfully presented these issues to the world.

This book, however, is not a statistical journal. What you will find are the results presented in a most informative and, yes, opinionated manner. The editors of QBR gathered the numerous responses, selected the titles most often cited, and supplemented them with our own recommendations. We then categorized those books into sections we believe speak directly to the heart of our matters: Origins, Ancestors, and Memory; Community and Identity; Politics, Nationalism, and Revolution; Soul and Spirit; Sisters' Stories; Brothers' Lives. Our final step was to offer brief commentary on each book, summarizing its plot or thesis, talking about what makes it special, and placing it, whenever possible, within the context of its time.

I have often spoken about the way interest in our books has historically waxed and waned. It would be easy to say that every thirty years since the mid-1800s, the beginning of Reconstruction, there has been a spike of interest in the literary affairs of the "Negro." Following the international interest in Frederick Douglass's freedom cry, the writing of Booker T. Washington held sway; Charles Chestnutt and Paul Laurence Dunbar were the anointed of the 1900s; Alain Locke ushered in Harlem's New Negro Movement in the late 1920s and early 1930s; Amiri Baraka, Haki Madhubuti, and Sonia Sanchez *slapped!* us to consciousness as the Black Arts Movement spread Stokely's fire in the 1960s; Sheharazod Ali's *The Black Man's Guide to Understanding the Black Woman* was the flint, and Terry McMillan's *Disappearing Acts* was the fire of the 1990s commercial renaissance.

In fact, every resurgent period of interest in African American literature corresponds to intense social changes. The Civil War marked the voluntary conscription and arming of a previously enslaved population; the mass migration of a disenfranchised public followed. The development of an urbane African American cultural aesthetic was followed by a call to black power. Today's literature reflects the economic and social progress wrought from Malcolm, Martin, urban unrest, open-door policies, and affirmative action. Accommodation and demand, protest and personal introspection mark this current period of African American literature.

Still, what we hoped to identify within this book were not only the books that serve as the literary landmarks of our social movements but also those critical and illuminating works that, due to the social stillness of the moment, fell quietly from the shelves yet survived by dint of word of mouth alone. We also wanted to add representative books from our brothers and sisters in Africa and the Caribbean, whose experiences have so closely paralleled the experiences of African Americans.

We anticipate that arguments will be made around the inclusion or exclusion of one book or another within this list of the essential one hundred. This, too, is part of our process. For certainly, when one discusses essential African American books, one can easily surpass one hundred.

Still, I would be remiss in not recommending Toni Cade Bambara's *Gorilla, My Love*, Wole Soyinka's *Ake*, Gayle Jones's *Corregidora*, and Paul Beatty's *White Boy Shuffle* or Sapphire's *Push*, both stylistic breakthrough novels of the '90s. These, too, should be enjoyed.

A number of noteworthy books that direct readers through African American literary history can be found in bookstores and libraries. The most recent of those, the *Norton Anthology of African American Literature*, joins the *Oxford Companion to African American Literature* and Howard University Press's *The New Cavalcade: African American Writing from 1760 to the Present, Vols. I* and *II*, as excellent primers to our world in literature. Those anthologies, along with this book, support a strong argument for the recognition of an African American literary canon, a functional canon that serves as a respite—a community safehouse—to which to turn when the going gets rough. Yes, the books in our canon must work as literature, but they must also reach the heart. And they must speak to communal truths.

The *Webster's Seventh New Collegiate Dictionary* definition of canon as "a criterion or standard of judgment" begs the question, Whose standards? What cultural criteria are to be met in order to gain inclusion within the list of books deemed "authoritative"? This will continue as a hotly debated issue, given the continuing shift in the American population, the "browning" of the American classroom, and the increasing number of culturally diverse voices being brought to print. Perhaps it is time to develop a more functional, world literary canon—a more inclusive and accepted body of work that serves cultures individually and nurtures a sense of community globally.

African American literature is the story of the African in the new Americas. It is a history of a people in transition and inner turmoil as we seek, still, to find a place within a society that has institutionalized its efforts to relegate blackness to its bottom rung. Ours, then, is an autobiography of protest and struggle for recognition, of achievement and survival.

Our earliest achievements in public letters and writings, protestations to enslavement, were autobiographical: the slave narrative. Even then, and beyond the telling of their plight, the writing was an attempt at proving an intellectual and moral capability and, by extension, the humanity of the enslaved African. Even the reality of post-Reconstruction and the advent of a covert American apartheid could not dim our urge to freedom.

And so with emancipation, we packed our belongings, knowing that if only the opportunity existed, we would show we were possessed of the will to thrive. To St. Louis, Chicago, New York, and all points north, east, and west, we migrated in search of better lives as free women and men, free to grow as a community, free as individuals to contribute to the ideal that was America.

It is from this community history that QBR selects the one hundred most representative books within the African experience in the Americas—books that are significant in that they represent visions and aspirations, or a turning in thought, attitude, or perspective within our evolution as citizens in the New World.

And because they mark the passage of our time on this earth, because they contain our parents' wisdom and ours, because they validate our sense of *I am,* and because they leave an indelible record of our contribution to the cultures of the world, we deem them essential both to us and to those who follow. We encourage you to create your own personal list of books so that you may pass our selections, along with yours, on to your friends and loved ones. Our compilation of the books with the greatest impact on us will be a project that lasts into the new millennium; we will continue to record these works on our web site (www.QBR.com). We would be honored to post your favorites. E-mail us or reach us by post.

May you read and prosper. We continue . . .

—Max Rodriguez

Origins, Ancestors, and Memory

Commentary

by Charles Brooks

The late John Henrik Clarke, in his essay "Why Africana History," stated: "History, I have often said, is a clock that people use to tell their political time of day. It is also a compass that people use to find themselves on the map of human geography. History tells a people where they have been and what they have been. It also tells a people where they are and what they are. Most importantly, history tells a people where they still must go and what they still must be." Dr. Clarke powerfully underlined the importance of grasping and understanding African and African American history because of its connection to the collective fate of a people. Simply put, "If you don't know your past, you don't know your future."

Writers from throughout the African Diaspora have created—and not without struggle—an impressive body of work documenting their origins as a people and reclaiming their right to remember the past. This has been one of the central functions of African American literature. Why has this task been so important? Because our history has often been erased, misrepresented, and used as a tool against us, when in fact it should be the most powerful tool of our empowerment. The truths of our history have been twisted and threatened with extinction—a situation that should be as lamentable to other peoples of the world as it is to people of African descent. Why? Because the real story of our origins, our ancestors, and our quest to remember is a compelling and, ultimately, deeply inspiring story—a gift bequeathed by our finest writers to us and to the world.

This section, "Origins, Ancestors, and Memory," profiles and excerpts nineteen works, spanning two hundred years. These

9

works speak volumes about who we were and who we are, and they provide a vision for what we have yet to achieve. They also provide an opportunity to share the hopes and dreams, pains and sorrows of our ancestors. The section begins by profiling two vital slave narratives, the first literary device used by African Americans to tell their story: *The Interesting Narrative of the Life of Olaudah Equiano* by Olaudah Equiano, and the redoubtable *Narrative of the Life and Times of Frederick Douglass* by Frederick Douglass. It also includes two of the earliest works of fiction created by African Americans, *Clotel* by William Wells Brown and *Our Nig* by Harriet E. Wilson. These early literary efforts were created as a response against the oppressive social institution of slavery. These books do more than retell the familiar story of slavery—they tell it from the perspective of the men and women who lived through it, who felt the pain of bondage and abuse, and who, instead of crumbling, took pen and paper in hand to speak out and make sure the horrible truth would not be ignored or forgotten.

Also profiled are works of history that chronicle the experiences of Africans from the earliest civilizations of antiquity to the contemporary era. Works such as John Hope Franklin's *From Slavery to Freedom*, Lerone Bennett's *Before the Mayflower*, and Ivan Van Sertima's controversial *They Came Before Columbus*, pioneering works of history that describe the varied experiences of people of African descent—not just the story of recent oppressions. Other works in this section speak to the need of black people interpreting the African and the African Diaspora historical experience for themselves. Included in this category is the seminal classic *Stolen Legacy* by George James.

Finally, the section includes works from contemporary writers of fiction who have taken on the work of remembering and rehumanizing our ancestors by reimagining their lives and struggles through highly imaginative storytelling techniques. Toni Morrison's heartbreaking *Beloved*, David Bradley's *The Chaneysville*

Incident, and Octavia Butler's startling *Kindred* are three splendid examples of this act of creative remembrance at work.

This collection of books articulates the commitment that people of African descent have made to document their historical experience in their own words. These books are tools we can all use to advance our understanding of humanity. Enjoy!

Charles Brooks is a freelance journalist and writer. He contributes to the New York Amsterdam News, The Source, The Black World Today, *and the* Black Collegian.

The Interesting Narrative of the Life of Olaudah Equiano, or Gustavus Vassa, the African, Written by Himself (1789)

Olaudah Equiano
Memoir

Published in England in 1789 and in the United States in 1791, *The Interesting Narrative of the Life of Olaudah Equiano* was the first slave narrative to be written without the aid of a ghostwriter or an editor. The clear, intelligent, and ardent voice of Equiano was among the first African voices to tell the story of the journey from Africa to America; his autobiography is considered the father of the slave narrative, the first literary form that black folks used to have their say.

Unlike most other slave narratives, Equiano begins his story in Africa—the idyllic land of his youth. He offers a detailed account of African cultural life and society prior to the European encroachment. Africa was a land "rich and fruitful" whose inhabitants were simple, noble, and in love with life: "We are almost a nation of dancers, musicians, and poets." His rose-tinged memories of a bright and humane existence in Africa are followed by descriptions of the agonies brought on by encounters with brutish and fearsome Europeans: war, the atrocity of the Middle Passage, and enslavement. By juxtaposing the peaceful, humane, and progressive land of his birth with the crude, animal-like behavior of the Europeans, Equiano flipped the script on the usual expectations of his primarily white audience, who typically assumed *they* were the civilized ones. As his story continued, Equiano stressed the importance of hard work (he purchased his own freedom with money he earned) and the crucial role of Christian faith in his life.

This first manifestation of the African American genius for autobiography—a genius that would later give us the lives of Frederick Douglass, Malcolm X, Maya Angelou, and countless others in their own words—gave eloquent voice to the experience of the voiceless millions who made the journey from Africa to America. And like the memorable books produced by Frederick, Malcolm, and Maya, Equiano's book is both a fascinating tale and a story with a mission: to describe and protest the enslaved condition of his people. Pre-dating Frederick Douglass's *Narrative of the Life of Frederick Douglass, an American Slave* by some fifty years, Olaudah Equiano's *Life* did for abolitionists in Great Britain what Douglass's *Narrative* did for the movement in the United States: It exposed the horrors of slavery while simultaneously holding the mirror of blame to the European, and it lent a human face to enslaved Africans, around which a slave reform movement could develop. As much a surprise to the world as it was "interesting," its passion and quality of prose made it the most influential literary work by an African American in the eighteenth century.

The Narrative of the Life and Times of Frederick Douglass: An American Slave, Written by Himself (1845)

Frederick Douglass

Memoir

W hen it was first published, many critics doubted that *The Narrative of the Life and Times of Frederick Douglass* had even been written by Frederick Douglass. As odd as it may seem now, that criticism was not completely unfounded: In the mid-nineteenth century, the antislavery movement produced hundreds of slave narratives, many of them ghostwritten by white abolitionists and tailored to create sympathy for their movement. But this book, by this remarkable man, was different. The tag line at the end of the book's subtitle—*Written by Himself*—was vitally important. Although clearly written with the abolitionist cause in mind, this book is not merely a political tract. True, its dispassionate prose brought to light the "injustice, exposure to outrage, and savage barbarity" of slavery as Douglass observed and experienced it. But it also brought to life an uncommon man and the particular concerns seared into him during his experience of bondage. Douglass recounts that during slavery, he and his people were denied life's fundamentals: faith, family, education, the capacity for bold action, a sense of community, and personal identity. Douglass saw reclamation of these things as the key to his and his people's survival, redemption, and salvation.

The autobiography opens with a description of the aspects of his own life that Douglass was never allowed to know: the identity of his father, the warmth and care of his mother (who was a stranger to him), and even the fact of his own date of birth. As a child, he suffered from and observed savage beatings firsthand, including the fierce beating of his Aunt Hester at the hands of their master, Captain Aaron Anthony. As he grew older, Douglass liberated himself in stages: mentally, spiritually, and, eventually, physically. His mental freedom began when he was taught to read and write and realized the power of literacy; his spiritual freedom came when he discovered the grace of Christianity and the will to resist his beatings; his physical freedom arrived when he finally escaped to the North.

After escaping, Douglass was committed to telling the world about the condition of the brothers and sisters he left behind. Aside from telling Douglass's personal story, his autobiography takes us to the fields and the cabins and the lives of many slaves to reveal the real human cost of slavery. Douglass focused on the dehumanizing aspects of slavery: not just the beatings, but the parting of children from their mothers, the denial of education, and the sexual abuses of slave masters. He ends the book with this statement: "Sincerely and earnestly hoping that his little book may do something toward throwing light on the American slave system, and hastening the glad day of deliverance to the millions of my brethren in bonds—faithfully relying upon the power of truth, love, and justice, for success in my humble efforts—and solemnly pledgeing myself anew to the sacred cause, I subscribe myself, Frederick Douglass."

The book was an incredible success: It sold over thirty thousand copies and was an international bestseller. It was the first, and most successful, of three autobiographies that Douglass was to write. The other two, *My Bondage and My Freedom* (1855) and *The Life and Times of Frederick Douglass,* update the story of his life and revise some of the facts of his earlier autobiography.

Clotel: or, The President's Daughter, A Narrative of Slave Life in the United States (1853)

William Wells Brown
Novel

After his 1834 escape from slavery, William Wells Brown became a noted activist, orator, journalist, and memoirist in the cause of abolition. When he published *Clotel; or, The President's Daughter* nineteen years after his escape, he also became the first African American novelist. *Clotel* was a complicated mix of literary genres—part melodrama, part escape narrative, part love story—but it is not surprising that the first African American novel was first and foremost a novel of political protest, a genre that would be well-tread by Brown's literary progeny.

Clotel was also the first abolitionist novel produced by a black man who had himself escaped bondage, so Brown's exhaustive chronicling of the shameful behavior of white Americans in the face of slavery is written with knowing detail and passion. Brown named names and pulled no punches, denouncing the hypocrisy of religion and democracy, clergymen and politicians. He also explored troubling themes that have recurred throughout African American literary history: color envy among African Americans, the exploitation of black women, the struggles of nurturing a black family under oppressive conditions, and the maddening chasm between the ideals of American democracy and freedom and the reality of black life in America.

The novel tells several stories (in fact, it opens with Brown's own story of escape) but primarily follows the life of Clotel, the enslaved daughter of Thomas Jefferson and his mulatto house-maid, Currer. The novel opens with Clotel, her mother, and her

sister Althesa being sold on the auction block to different masters. Clotel is sold to Horatio Green and becomes his concubine.
She develops a genuine emotional attachment to Green and has
his child, Mary. When Green marries, his new wife forces him to
sell Clotel while retaining Mary. The novel then follows Clotel's
exciting escape from her new master, from Mississippi to Louis-
ville, Cincinnati, Richmond, and, finally, Washington, D.C., where
the novel's final drama unfolds in the shadow of the nation's
Capitol.

The assertion that Jefferson had children with his enslaved
mistresses was so controversial that the complete, unexpurgated
version of the book was not published in the United States until
1969. Wells released the book in several editions and under different titles during his lifetime, and although it never did achieve
the success of other antislavery novels published in the period,
notably *Uncle Tom's Cabin*, it has endured as one of the first
powerful fictional salvos in the ongoing battle for justice and
equality in this Land of the Free.

Even with her short hair, Clotel was handsome. Her life had been
a secluded one, and though now nearly thirty years of age, she
was still beautiful. At her short hair, the other servants laughed,
"Miss Clo needn't strut round so big, she got short nappy har
well as I," said Nell. . . . "She thinks she white, when she come
here wid that long har of hers," replied Mill. . . . The fairness of
Clotel's complexion was regarded with envy as well by the other
servants as by the mistress herself. This is one of the hard features
of slavery.

—from *Clotel*

Our Nig, or, Sketches from the Life of a Free Black, in a Two-Story White House, North (1859)

Harriet E. Wilson
Novel

I t is the relatively obscure writer Harriet E. Wilson who has earned the title of Mother of Black Women's Fiction. *Our Nig*, the first novel by an African American woman, transports the reader of the African experience in America to the North—the Promised Land—*freedom*. The time: circa 1859; the place: Boston, or its environs. Through Alfrado, the novel's female protagonist, Wilson adds to the American literary palette the first of many black heroines who evince moral rectitude and strength of character. But Alfrado's life was no crystal stair. As Wilson describes it, the "freedom" afforded blacks in the North was a chimera; the "shadows of slavery"—racist abuse, servitude, limited opportunity—fell hard on New England's black citizens and particularly hard on black women.

After the death of her father, a black man, Frado is abandoned by her white mother and her mother's new black lover. Frado becomes a servant for a white family, the Bellmonts. While Mr. Bellmont and his sons are kind-hearted men, Frado is chronically mistreated and tormented by Mrs. Bellmont, a diabolic woman intent on destroying Frado's spirit through scoldings and physical violence. Frado withstands the worst of Mrs. Bellmont and eventually rebels, refusing to be beaten, much to the shock of her mistress. She leaves the Bellmont household and eventually marries Samuel, a con man who claims to be a former slave and makes his living as an abolitionist orator. When Frado becomes pregnant, Samuel takes off, leaving her alone and in desperate poverty.

"Yes, *yes!* " she repeated sarcastically, "you know these niggers are just like black snakes; you *can't* kill them. If she wasn't tough she would have been killed long ago. There was never one of my girls could do half the work."

"Did they ever try?" interposed her husband. "I think she can do more than all of them together."

"What a man!" said she, peevishly. "But I want to know what is going to be done with her about getting pious?"

"Let her do just as she has a mind to. If it comforts her, let her enjoy the privilege of being good. I see no objection."

"I should think *you* were crazy, sure. Don't you know that every night she will want to go toting off to meeting? and Sundays, too? and you know we have a great deal of company Sundays, and she can't be spared."

"I thought you Christians held to going to church," remarked Mr. B.

"Yes, but who ever thought of having a nigger go, except to drive others there? Why, according to you and James, we should very soon have her in the parlor, as smart as our own girls. It's of no use talking to you or James. If you should go on as you would like, it would not be six months before she would be leaving me; and that won't do. Just think how much profit she was to us last summer. We had no work hired out; she did the work of two girls—"

"And got the whippings for two with it!" remarked Mr. Bellmont.

"I'll beat the money out of her, if I can't get her worth any other way," retorted Mrs. B. sharply.

—from *Our Nig*

It is at this point that Frado decides to write the story of her life. The novel ends on a poignant note, with Frado hopeful that sales of the book will allow her to care for her financial needs.

While it was a sentimental novel, *Our Nig* told a tough story in realistic and often strikingly beautiful language, without the melodrama or happy endings of contemporary novels and autobiographical narratives. In certain facets, Frado is a remarkably modern character: she was a working-class and ultimately independent woman who found spiritual strength in resistance. The clarity and realism with which Wilson rendered Frado may come from the fact that, in all likelihood, Frado's story was literally the story of Wilson's life. Wilson herself suffered for years as a servant to a difficult employer and was abandoned in pregnancy by a good-for-nothing con man and had to turn to writing to support herself. As noted by the editors of *The Norton Anthology of African American Literature*: "Thus African American women's fiction originated in necessity, if not virtual desperation, but took form and meaning in Wilson's eloquent testimony."

Up from Slavery (1901)

Booker T. Washington
Memoir

T he history of the African in America has often been per-
sonalized or embodied within one individual, one spokes-
person who represented the sentiments of the moment. In the
South of the 1890s, Booker T. Washington stood as the often controversial personification of the aspirations of the black masses.
The Civil War had ended, casting an uneducated black mass adrift
or, equally tenuous, creating a class of sharecroppers still dependent on the whims of their former owners. Black Reconstruction,
for all its outward trimming, had failed to deliver its promised
economic and political empowerment. While an embittered and
despairing black population sought solace and redemption, a
white citizenry systematically institutionalized racism.

From this Armageddon rose this Moses, Booker Taliaferro
Washington, who was born in 1856 in Virginia, of a slave mother
and a white father he never knew. But he gave no indication in his
autobiography of the pain this almost certainly caused him: "I do
not even know his name. I have heard reports to the effect that
he was a white man who lived on one of the nearby plantations.
But I do not find especial fault with him. He was simply another
unfortunate victim of the institution which the nation unhappily
had engrafted upon it at that time." After Emancipation, Washington began to dream of getting an education and resolved to go to
the Hampton Normal Agricultural Institute in Virginia. When he
arrived, he was allowed to work as the school's janitor in return for
his board and part of his tuition. After graduating from Hampton,
Washington was selected to head a new school for blacks at Tuskegee, Alabama, where he taught the virtues of "patience, thrift,
good manners and high morals" as the keys to empowerment.

An unabashed self-promoter (Tuskegee was dependent upon the largesse of its white benefactors) and advocate of accommodation, Washington's "pick yourself up by your bootstraps" and "be patient and prove yourself first" philosophy was simultaneously acclaimed by the masses, who prescribed to self-reliance, and condemned by the black intelligentsia, who demanded a greater and immediate inclusion in the social, political, and economic fabric of this emerging nation. Washington's philosophy struck a chord that played like a symphony within the racial politics of the times. It gave a glimmer of hope to the black masses; it created for whites a much-needed locus for their veneer of social concern—funds flooded into Tuskegee Institute; and finally, the initiatives of the black intelligentsia, led by W. E. B. Du Bois, were, for the moment, neutralized.

Washington "believed that the story of his life was a typical American success story," and he redefined "success" to make it so: "I have learned that success is to be measured not so much by the position that one has reached in his life as by the obstacles which he has overcome while trying to succeed." His powerfully simple philosophy that self-help is the key to overcoming obstacles of racism and poverty has resonated among African Americans of all political stripes, from Marcus Garvey to Louis Farrakhan.

Ignorant and inexperienced, it is not strange that in the first years of our new life (after slavery) we began at the top instead of at the bottom; that a seat in Congress or the state legislature was more sought than real estate or industrial skill; . . . No race can prosper till it learns that there is as much dignity in tilling a field as in writing a poem. It is at the bottom of life we must begin, and not at the top.

—from *Up from Slavery*

Black Reconstruction in America: An Essay toward a History of the Part Which Black Folk Played in the Attempt to Reconstruct Democracy in America, 1860–1880 (1935)

W. E. B. Du Bois
History

In *Black Reconstruction in America*, Du Bois applies his keen eye to the question of America's post–Civil War Reconstruction, and why it failed. Emancipation for African Americans did not bring on a glorious new beginning for them. Besides not getting their promised forty acres and a mule, the former slaves were denied the vote, denied equal educational opportunities, and cheated out of their livelihood by the sharecropping system. Reconstruction, a never-to-be-repeated opportunity to genuinely change the nature of race relations in the South, only delayed the reestablishment of white dominance over the lives of black southerners.

The brilliantly written and exhaustively researched *Black Reconstruction in America* was completed in 1935 while black southerners still lived under the stifling reign of Jim Crow. Du Bois considered this work to be his magnum opus. In addition to cataloging the reversals of the post-Reconstruction South, Du Bois presented Reconstruction as a lost opportunity for all Americans. He describes the Civil War, the emancipation of slaves, and Reconstruction as being part of a dramatic revolutionary movement that created, for an all-too-brief historical moment, true democracy in America. And he portrays African Americans as bold actors in that drama, rather than as just passively manipulated pawns in the power games of northern and southern whites. But in the end, he insisted that equal rights for blacks were still missing from American society. Du Bois used strong language and commonsense reasoning to make the case that even under the best circumstances, it would take black people time to shake off the effects of slavery, but in a still-hostile South and without the protection of the American government, it was insanity to expect blacks to make quick advancements.

In *Black Reconstruction,* Du Bois points to the failures of Reconstruction to adequately reconstruct American society so that its black citizens could move forward fully enfranchised and with equal rights under the law. *Black Reconstruction* gives a penetrating analysis of how Reconstruction fell short of creating true democracy for all Americans and instead began a new process of discrimination and disenfranchisement for free black citizens. The effects of America's failure to live up to its promises and ideals are still being felt by its people—both black and white.

The unending tragedy of Reconstruction is the utter inability of the American mind to grasp its real significance, its national and world-wide implications. . . . We apparently expected that this social upheaval was going to be accomplished with peace, honesty and efficiency, and that the planters were going to quietly surrender the right to live on the labor of black folk, after two hundred and fifty years of habitual exploitation. And it seems to America a proof of inherent race inferiority that four million slaves did not completely emancipate themselves in eighty years, in the midst of nine million bitter enemies, and indifferent public opinion of the whole nation. If the Reconstruction of the Southern states, from slavery to free labor, and from aristocracy to industrial democracy, had been conceived as a major national program of America, whose accomplishment at any price was well worth the effort, we should be living today in a different world.

—from *Black Reconstruction*

From Slavery to Freedom: A History of African Americans (1947)

John Hope Franklin

History

Writing in the *New Republic* about the scholarly contribution of historian John Hope Franklin, the late Roy Wilkins noted, "John Hope Franklin is an uncommon historian who has consistently corrected, in clear, vigorous language, the misreading of this country's rich heritage." Similarly complimentary is the more recent assessment by historian Nell Irvin Painter, who praised Franklin for his "great intellectual integrity" and open identification of himself "as a black person concerned with black people." The combination of rigorous, authoritative scholarship and unabashed affection that Franklin brought to his subject—his people—remains the standard by which subsequent histories have been judged.

From Slavery to Freedom, originally published in 1947, was in its seventh edition in 1999. It is usually referred to as the authoritative history of African Americans. Beginning with the pre-Diasporic African states and institutions, the narrative follows the African "forced migration" to the Caribbean, the early American colonies, and Latin America. The major focus of the text is, of course, on the United States. Recent editions have brought the African American experience through to the Black Revolution of the 60s and 70s and expanded the coverage of African states and contemporary issues. Its in-depth discussion of slavery remains one of the most authoritative accounts of the "peculiar institution."

Franklin once said, "It was necessary, as a black historian, to have a personal agenda." At the same time, his history has remained redoubtable over the years, in part owing to his politically objective point of view. From its first edition through its current incarnation, the book never adhered to the fashionable ideology of the day, whether Marxism or Afrocentrism, but let the history speak for itself. In fact, historian Earle Thorpe has noted that at its initial publication in 1947, there were mixed reactions to the work from the black intellectual community. He concedes, however, that despite the conventionality of its content and interpretation, "the objectivity of the author, his temperateness in tone, thorough grasp of his materials, and scholarly presentation make the work a significant contribution." Not a radical history, but thorough, durable, and essential.

Stolen Legacy (1954)

George G. M. James
Nonfiction

Stolen Legacy stands among the first scholarly works that have attempted to recover the "lost" history of early African civilization. George G. M. James was a professor of Latin, Greek, and mathematics. It was his interest in the roots of Greek philosophy and the seemingly "immaculate conception of Western civilization" that brought him to ask such questions as Who were the Greek scholars? Who were their teachers? How did what they learned fit into the contemporary Greek worldview? And, when James considered the fates of the greatest of them—Anaxagoras was imprisoned and exiled, Socrates executed, Plato sold into slavery, and Aristotle exiled—he wondered why they were considered to be undesirable citizens in their own land.

Could it be that Greek philosophers were so mistreated because they imported a foreign and therefore subversive worldview? For example, Pythagoras, the "father of geometry" and the first Greek philosopher, was purported to have traveled to Egypt. He settled in Italy and practiced a simple, communal life, the goal of which was to live in harmony with the divine. To that end, he prescribed a regimen of purification that included dietary restrictions and periods of silence and contemplation. He taught the kinship of all life and the immortality and transmigration of the soul.

Stolen Legacy argues that Greek philosophers were not the originators of Greek philosophy, but that they derived it from Egyptian priests. James posits that Greece during this period of "enlightenment" was, in fact, constantly engaged in war and internal conflict, creating an environment not conducive to the evolution of philosophy. He bluntly states that Greek philosophy was the offspring of the Egyptian Mystery System and that the Egyptians educated the Greeks.

Upon its publication in 1954, *Stolen Legacy* was not well received; however, it has remained in print to this day as a controversial chronicle of the possible African origins of classical civilization. Even if you don't agree with all of James's conclusions, the questions he asks and the theories he asserts are fascinating to anyone interested in studying classical civilizations from an African-centered perspective.

Before the Mayflower (1966, latest rev. ed., 1988)

Lerone Bennett Jr.

History

*B*efore the Mayflower grew out of a series of articles Bennett published in *Ebony* magazine in 1962, regarding "the trials and triumphs of a group of Americans whose roots in the American soil are deeper than the roots of the Puritans who arrived on the celebrated *Mayflower* a year after a 'Dutch man of war' deposited twenty Negroes at Jamestown." Bennett's history is infused with a desire to set the record straight about black contributions to the Americas and about the powerful Africans of antiquity. While not a fresh history, it provides a solid synthesis of current historical research and a lively writing style that makes it accessible and engaging reading.

After discussing the contributions of Africans to the ancient world, *Before the Mayflower* tells the history of "the other Americans," how they came to America, and what happened to them when they got here. The book is comprehensive and detailed, providing little-known and often overlooked facts about the lives of black folks through slavery, Reconstruction, America's wars, the Great Depression, and the civil rights movement. The book includes a useful time line and some fascinating archival images.

Bennett, who attended Morehouse College, was a reporter in Mississippi before becoming the first senior editor of *Ebony*. He has published several books on the black experience, as well as a biography of Martin Luther King Jr. Bennett hoped to astonish the reader with "the richness of the Negro's heritage," to illustrate that their story is "relevant to the struggle of all men." With *Before the Mayflower*, he succeeded brilliantly.

Civilization started in the great valleys of Africa and Asia. Blacks, or people who would be considered blacks today, were among the first people to use tools, paint pictures, plant seeds and worship gods. In the beginning, black people marched in the front ranks of the emerging human procession. They founded empires and states. They made some of the critical discoveries and contributions that led to the modern world.

—from *Before the Mayflower*

Two Thousand Seasons (1976)

Ayi Kwei Armah

Novel

"That we the black people are one people we know. Destroyers will travel long distances in their minds and out to deny you this truth. We do not argue with them, the fools. Let them presume to instruct us about ourselves. That too is in their nature. That too is in the flow of their two thousand seasons against us." With this searing indictment, Ayi Kwei Armah tells us of the way of our ancestors, and of our prophesied two-thousand-year walk in the valley of the destroyers.

How often have we looked for some direction, some inkling of information regarding our ways advent to the Great Intrusion, that period prior to our open-armed welcome of the Muslim hoard? How often have we sought some glimmer, some fraction of insight into ancient societal Africa and the communal spirit, our birthright, which guides us silently through resistance and survival?

Entwining fable and fact, Armah delivers both a saddening and a scathing account of our fall from grace. He tells, also, of the way that we left behind: "Our way is reciprocity. The way is wholeness. Our way knows no oppression. The way destroys oppression. Our way is hospitable to our guests. The way repels destroyers. Our way produces before it consumes. The way produces far more than it consumes. Our way creates. The way destroys only destruction."

Armah spares no one in his indictment. In our treason, black people too are guilty. If there is only one book within this collection that one must read, this is it.

They Came Before Columbus (1976)

Ivan Van Sertima

History

According to standard history, the first African Americans emerged from the holds of slave ships, shackled, confused, and already defeated by their European masters. *They Came Before Columbus* is a compelling, detailed, and exhaustively researched documentation of the presence and legacy of black Africans in America before Columbus. Van Sertima, an anthropological historian from Rutgers University who is also a gifted writer, painstakingly sifts the documentation of centuries of research into a cohesive narrative that aims to prove that Africans predated Columbus in America and that their contributions as artisans, agricultural scientists, and linguists are still seen in present-day America.

Van Sertima's controversial claims stem from historical, navigational, archeological, linguistic, oral, and botanical evidence of a pre-Columbian African presence in the Americas. Van Sertima cites Indian words and religious and cultural practices apparently derived from the Mandingos and other African nations. Records indicate that Indians spoke of trading with Africans. Oral histories from West African griots talk of expeditions across the Atlantic. American nicotine and cocaine have been found in the bodies of entombed Egyptians. And there were even confirmed sightings by European explorers, including Vasco Nuñez de Balboa, who allegedly stumbled across African prisoners of war in an Indian camp, and the Spanish priest Fray Gregorio García, who wrote, "Here we found slaves of the lord—Negroes—who were the first our people saw in the Indies."

Van Sertima's work has come under fire from numerous critics. But each reader can draw his or her own conclusions based on the provocative and truly fascinating evidence presented here. A work of great importance and popularity, *They Came Before Columbus* argues that it was Africans who crossed the Atlantic first and that those ingenious first "African Americans" left behind tantalizing clues of their presence.

The Mande people of West Africa created a center of plant domestication around the headwaters of the river Niger circa 4500 B.C. Black Africans contributed the bottle gourd, the watermelon, the tamarind fruit and cultivated cotton to Egypt. . . . Black gods and gods with Negro features have been found among the American Indians. It is hard for many to imagine the Negro-African figure being venerated as a god. He has always been represented as the lowliest of the low, at least since the era of conquest and slavery. His humiliation as a world figure begins, in fact, with the coming of Columbus. The Negro-African as a backward, slow and uninventive being is still with us . . . the memory of his cultural and technological achievements before the day of his humiliation seem to have been erased from the consciousness of history.

—from *They Came Before Columbus*

Roots: The Saga of an American Family
(1976)

Alex Haley
Novel

Roots is the fictionalized account of Alex Haley's family history and an epic narrative of the African American experience. For many African Americans, the novel and the history-making television miniseries it begot were pivotal in their understanding and appreciation of their origins. The story traces Haley's family history from the imagined birth of his ancestor Kunta Kinte in an African village in 1750 to the death, seven generations later, of his father in Arkansas. Based on fifteen years of research by Haley, the novel is a combination of fact and fiction—it is often referred to as faction—that puts a human face on the suffering of black people through the ordeal of the Middle Passage, slavery, and Jim Crow. Its combination of compelling, affectionate storytelling and informative history has had a revolutionary effect on the way Americans—black and white—think about the history of a people.

The story, like that of Olaudah Equiano, begins in an idyllic African world destroyed by Europeans. Haley's description of Kinte's journey to America in the hold of a slave ship is harrowing and indelibly memorable. Kinte is enslaved in America but is still proud, refusing to forsake his African name or heritage. He passes on stories of Africa to his daughter, Kizzy, who bears a child, Chicken George. George is a successful cockfighter whose father is also his master—a common situation in the time of slavery but one that is treated with unusual sensitivity here. George passes the stories of his grandfather on to his children, including Tom, who marries a part-Indian woman named Irene. Tom and Irene have eight children, one of whom is Haley's grandmother.

She passes the family stories to her daughter, who passes them on to Haley. Haley, in turn, tells the story, from Kunta Kinte to Chicken George, to his own grandmother, to his children.

Haley has been accused of plagiarism and his book has been criticized for historical inaccuracies, but the novel holds up as a powerful representation of the full African American saga. Haley tells the story of his family—and, by extension, the story of all black people whose family histories are lost in the mists of time— with an immense amount of respect and tenderness. Amidst the undeniable misery of slavery and Jim Crow, he always reveals the outstanding characteristics that sustained his family—spirited resistance, cunning survival instincts, and a will to remember and pass on. James Baldwin captured the book's appeal when he wrote, "Alex Haley's taking us back through time to the village of his ancestors is an act of faith and courage, but this book is also an act of love, and it is this which makes it haunting."

Sally Hemings (1979)

Barbara Chase-Riboud
Novel

Almost twenty years ago, Barbara Chase-Riboud made literary history when she published *Sally Hemings*. The novel spent six weeks on the *New York Times* best-seller list, sold 1.6 million copies worldwide, and breathed life into an historical enigma.

Sally Hemings details one of the greatest and most controversial stories in America: the tempestuous love affair between Thomas Jefferson, third president of the United States, and his quadroon slave, the extravagantly beautiful Sally Hemings. Epic in proportion yet rendered in exquisite detail by a writer with the eye of a historian and the heart of a storyteller, Barbara Chase-Riboud illustrates the story of Sally Hemings—Thomas Jefferson's half-stepsister, mistress, the mother of his children, and the slave he would never set free.

Sally had lived happily at Monticello, the Jefferson plantation in Virginia, for many years. It was when she was sent to join the Jeffersons in Paris, when she was fourteen and Thomas forty-four, that he fell hopelessly in love with her. "The return to Virginia and to slavery had been a shock to me. In Paris, we had both forgotten what it meant to be white or black, master or slave."

By chronicling the tempestuous lives of two families, one black and one white yet both inextricably linked, *Sally Hemings* shows irrefutably one of the prime peculiarities of the peculiar institution: that love and bondage often went hand in hand.

She had never contemplated freedom. Freedom, to Sally Hemings, was a vague, glimmering place no one ever returned from to prove it really existed.

—from *Sally Hemings*

The Chaneysville Incident (1981)

David Bradley
Novel

D avid Bradley's second book, *The Chaneysville Incident*, took ten years to complete. A deeply moving work set in the mountains of Pennsylvania, it received the PEN/Faulkner Award as the best novel of 1981. John Washington, the novel's hero, is a history professor and scholar, a man with an impressive mastery of his academic world, a proud rebuke to stereotypes of black intellectual inferiority. But he is utterly detached from his heritage; he is a historian of other people's history who wants to believe that his identity as a black man goes no further than the color of his skin. John is nevertheless driven by circumstances and his own demons to go back home, to the mountains of Pennsylvania, and back in time, to the lives of his ancestors, to uncover the truth about his father and his father's father and, ultimately, about himself.

The novel opens with Washington, the consummate professional whose demons are well contained deep within his subconscious, having reached a critical point in his life. His girlfriend, Judith, demands a greater emotional commitment, which he finds he is unable to give. When he is summoned back to the town of his birth by an urgent message advising him of the imminent death of Old Jack, the only one of the three men who reared him still living, he begins an introspective journey that challenges his willingness and ability to expiate his demons. With the help of the dying Jack, he enters a personal history he had staunchly avoided because of an emotionally inaccessible father and the contempt that he holds for his mother. Washington uncovers the mystery of his father's suicide; learns the heroic truth of how his great-grandfather, an ex-slave, was killed when caught helping twelve runaways; discovers that his contempt for his mother is misplaced; and creates within himself a place of compassion where commitment to Judith can grow.

The heroes of *The Chaneysville Incident*—John Washington; his father, Moses; and his grandfather, Brobdingnag C. K.—stand apart as strong, contemplative, intellectual men. Each, in his own way, uses tools of logic and creativity to invent ways of understanding and surviving in an illogical, hostile world. But they are also men who draw their strength from and give their lives for family, community, and heritage. As John grows up, his disconnection from family, community, and heritage lead him to an unbalanced life—strong intellect, malnourished spirit—and a tormented psyche. In beautiful and precise prose, Bradley tells the story of how that balance between intellect and spirit was regained, and how an intelligent reclamation of one's heritage can be a source of strength and peace.

Beloved (1987)

Toni Morrison
Novel

W hen Toni Morrison was an editor at Random House, she edited *The Black Book,* an anthology/scrapbook of African American history. While working on the book, she ran across a newspaper article about a woman named Margaret Garner, a runaway slave who killed her children, slitting the throat of one and bashing in the skull of the other, to prevent them from being recaptured by the slave hunters hot on their trail. This upside-down story of motherly love expressed through child murder haunted Morrison for many years and finally manifest itself in fictional form in her Pulitzer Prize–winning fifth novel, *Beloved.* A poetic chronicle of slavery and its aftermath, it describes how that inhuman ordeal forced cruel choices and emotional pain on its victims and gave them memories that would possess them long after they were released from their physical bondage. Morrison uses the story to address a key question for black people then and now: How can we let go of the pain of the past and redeem the sacrifices made in the struggle for freedom?

The novel's main character, Sethe, escapes from a plantation where she was viciously abused and perversely cherished by her master for her "skills" as a childbearer. When the slave hunters come looking for her, she kills her infant child to prevent her from becoming a slave. After slavery, Sethe finds work and devotes herself to her surviving daughter, Denver, but is haunted by memories of cruel life on the plantation she escaped and by the vindictive spirit of her murdered infant, Beloved. Paul D., an almost supernaturally charming former slave from the same plantation as Sethe, arrives and temporarily banishes the ghost of the infant Beloved. But Beloved returns in an older and more dan-

Not even trying, [Paul D.] had become the kind of man who could walk into a house and make the women cry. Because with him, in his presence, they could. There was something blessed in his manner. Women saw him and wanted to weep—to tell him that their chest hurt and their knees did too. Strong women and wise saw him and told him things they only told each other: that way past the Change of Life, desire in them had suddenly become enormous, greedy, more savage than when they were fifteen, and that it embarrassed them and made them sad; that secretly they longed to die—to be quit of it—that sleep was more precious to them than any waking day. Young girls sidled up to him to confess or describe how well-dressed the visitations were that had followed them straight from their dreams. Therefore, although he did not understand why this was so, he was not surprised when Denver dripped tears into the stovefire. Nor, fifteen minutes later, after telling him about her stolen milk, her mother wept as well. Behind her, bending down, his body an arc of kindness, he held her breasts in the palms of his hands.

—from *Beloved*

gerous form and sets out to destroy Sethe's household by seducing Paul D., driving Denver away from her mother, and feeding on Sethe's body and spirit.

Beloved is both beautiful and elusive: beautiful for its powerful and captivating language, and elusive not just because of its reliance on visions of haints and apparitions, but in its narrative interweaving of the past and present, the physical and the spiritual. For all of its supernatural elements, however, *Beloved* is most notable as a powerful tribute to the real-life struggles of a generation of black men and women to reconcile the horrors of the past and move on. The spirit of Beloved and the recurring memories of the tribulations Sethe endured on the plantations she lived on and escaped from were both testaments to the tangibly powerful hold that slavery had on her. In the end, she is able to recover her life only by finding within herself and her community the spiritual tools strong enough to exorcise her of this haunting. In this, Sethe's struggle is the struggle of all African Americans: the struggle to redeem ourselves, our families, and our communities from the wreckage of the past even as we honor the sacrifices made for survival.

Kindred (1988)

Octavia Butler
Novel

U sing the techniques of science fiction, Octavia Butler in
Kindred tangles in a startlingly unique and imaginative
way with some of the most fundamental questions about slavery:
How does one become mentally enslaved? What is the nature of
the slave-master relationship? What is the relevance of slavery to
modern-day descendants of slaves?

Dana Franklin, a black woman writer, is celebrating her
twenty-sixth birthday in 1976 when she is snatched from her
Southern California home and transported to the bank of a river
in the antebellum South where she saves the life of a young white
child who appears to be drowning. When the child's parents
arrive, they begin to beat Dana; when the child's father attempts
to shoot her, she is transported back to the twentieth century.
The child is Rufus Weylin, whom Dana later discovers is to be the
father of one of her ancestors, a child born of Weylin's rape of
Alice Greenwood, one of his slaves. Thus, the preservation of his
life is critical to Dana's survival. She is transported to the nineteenth century whenever his life is in danger, and she returns to
the twentieth century whenever *her* life is in danger.

She begins to develop an attachment to Rufus; in every life-
saving encounter with him, she attempts to teach him not to fall
into the racism endemic in his family and southern society. In
essence, she tries to save both his body and his soul. But her trips
back in time are too infrequent to have any lasting effect on
Weylin, who buys into the racist and sexist system that surrounds
him. Dana takes an interest in the Weylin slaves, particularly
Alice, and uses her literacy and knowledge of modern medical
skills to help them. But in order to guarantee her own existence

in the future, she also must encourage Alice to have sex with Rufus. Eventually, Dana too is made a slave and forced into an intimate understanding of the horrors of slavery and her own limitations.

The tension of the oddly symbiotic relationship between Dana and Weylin makes this book a riveting read. By transporting a modern-day African American woman into slavery, Butler vividly brings to life the hardships endured by the slaves. Dana frequently compares her strength and survival skills to those of the enslaved women and finds herself wanting. In the end, Dana finds the strength to break free of her physical slavery and the hold that the past has on her, while ensuring her own survival in the present, but she can never again forget the struggles of her exploited ancestors.

Spirits of the Passage: The Transatlantic Slave Trade in the Seventeenth Century
(1997)

Madeline Burnside and Rosemarie Robotham
Nonfiction

How can one sunken vessel represent three hundred years of history? Black scuba diver Mel Fisher's discovery of the *Henrietta Marie,* a slave ship that foundered off the coast of Florida in 1700, served as the inspiration for the writing of *Spirits of the Passage.* This sunken merchant slaver, with its many accoutrements of "the trade" still intact, became the earliest "living" monument to the greatest of all human crimes—the ownership and enslavement of humans for profit.

A beautifully illustrated book, *Spirits of the Passage* relates the history of the transatlantic slave trade through passages of narrative and attractive, informative photographs and drawings. It begins with an overview of the world circa 1400 that quickly dispels the myth of the Portuguese as the originators of the African slave trade. That ignoble honor belongs to the Moors of North Africa, a Berber people who in the mid-fifteenth century were Europe's main procurer of all races of slaves—black and eastern European alike.

Spirits of the Passage describes the antecedents to the transatlantic slave trade: the hegemonist philosophies of the Portuguese, the Spanish, the Dutch, and the English governments; the social and economic hardships of life in London that led to the English settlement of the New World; and the constant internecine warfare among African tribes, which made prisoners abundant, expendable, and available to meet the exploding demand for exported human labor. Tribal warfare, along with the avarice of some African elders, became the wedge used by Europeans to feed their expansionist greed.

The book then presents a description of the infamous Middle Passage, a harrowing history of survival, murder, acceptance, mutiny, and suicide. The book concludes with the arrival in the New World, and the rest, as they say, is (our) history. *Spirits of the Passage* is a deeply informative and engrossing book.

Community
and Identity

Commentary

by Robert Fleming

Community and *identity* are two of the most important criteria used to evaluate the humanity, potential, and spiritual worth of a people. Despite the political, economic, and social oppression that has plagued us since our forced introduction to these shores, our troubled march toward full equality in the face of overwhelming odds has been nurtured by our faith in our worth as individuals and our connection to each other. When protesters during the bloody southern civil rights campaigns of the mid-sixties carried signs reading I AM A MAN, every black person in America knew exactly what was being said. At that moment, we snatched back the power to define ourselves.

It was our sense of community, our blood-tie forged by ancestral love and mutual history, that provided us with the backbone to withstand our often brutal lives with an eye on the promised land of tomorrow. Our sense of a collective identity prevented us from completely falling victim to the powerful negative stereotypes and myths manufactured by the pro-slavery establishment. Our entrenched self-knowledge prevented us from buckling under the flood of pseudoscientific theories concocted to reduce our status to that of a childlike, primitive beast of burden. We never really believed we were niggers.

We knew it would not be easy to reverse bigoted views that many whites embraced and traced back to the Good Book and the tale of the Children of Ham. If you were not entirely human, how could you love your woman or children? How could you maintain a family? How could you appreciate the lush harmonies of music or admire the breathtaking beauty of a flower in full bloom? Or create anything of lasting wonder from your limited powers of reason and imagination?

We never really bought their Darwinian theories about us. If we had, we would no longer exist. We knew the truth. We knew how it felt to face indignity and injustice on a daily basis, we knew how it felt to be wounded on a spirit level, we knew what it meant to be an outsider. Yet we found ways to sustain ourselves. The mission of African American writers under these maddening circumstances has often been to use words as weapons in the war for self-definition, the war waged for the demise of Topsy, Sambo, and Uncle Tom. Writers included in this section of *Sacred Fire* fully understood this and structured their contributions to stress a deep commitment to truth and emotional honesty about our lives in a manner not commonly found in books written about us by whites.

The writers, in their dual roles of observer and interpreter, knew exactly what Claude McKay meant when he said "No white man could have written my books." Imagine Andrew Hacker or Studs Terkel, both considered astute chroniclers of our American experience, capturing the essence of black urban existence as sociologist St. Clair Drake did so aptly in his landmark study, *Black Metropolis: A Study of Negro Life in a Northern City*. Imagine any white writer assembling such a marvelous array of our finest Harlem Renaissance voices with the skill that editor Alain Locke achieved in his 1925 collection, *The New Negro*. Imagine Anne Tyler or Jane Smiley creating the complex relationship between Milkman Dead and his love-crazy cousin Hagar found in Toni Morrison's masterpiece *Song of Solomon*. Or Cheever or Updike conjuring up so realistically the struggle of Franchot to use the "square life" to escape the steely clutches of the ghetto in Richard Wright's riveting *Black Boy*.

Maybe Frantz Fanon, the sage observer from Martinique, explained it best in these few lines from his groundbreaking collection of essays *Black Skin, White Masks: The Experiences of a Black Man in a White World*: "I am black: I am the incarnation of a complete fusion with the world, an intuitive understanding of the earth, an abandonment of my ego in the heart of the cosmos, and no white man, no matter how intelligent he may be, can ever understand Louis Armstrong and the music of the Congo."

What Fanon is saying: Accept no substitutes. We can speak for ourselves. The real sound of Soul. The real style of Negritude. We know when it is real, no matter what the form, what the genre. If we browse the works of leading white science fiction writers such as Ray Bradbury, Philip K. Dick, or Ursula LeGuin, nothing there can compete with the blend of wise social commentary and poetic magic found in Octavia Butler's road novel *Kindred.* When Ralph Ellison takes us inside the helter-skelter consciousness of his narrator in his award-winning 1952 novel, *Invisible Man,* during his visit with Jim Trueblood, the black sharecropper, we see the question of identity and old racial myths handled with a sensibility foreign to the European aesthetic.

Just how much does identity matter? If there is any doubt as to whether McKay's statement rings true, a glimpse at this passage detailing the cry of the black soul from James Baldwin's highly accomplished first novel, *Go Tell It on the Mountain,* published in 1953, should set the record straight: ". . . And now in his moaning, and so far from any help, he heard it in himself—it rose from his bleeding, his cracked-open heart. It was a sound of rage and weeping which filled the grave, rage and weeping from time set free, but bound now in eternity; rage that had no language, weeping with no voice . . ." This is a cry that almost every black person afflicted with prolonged exposure to a hostile white world can understand.

In the years after slavery, Jim Crow and legalized segregation served as constant reminders to the descendants of the transplanted African of the bitter reality of color prejudice. Even today, after the changes brought on by the civil rights movement, the world can still be an unfriendly place, and in the minds of many, *a nigger is still a nigger,* regardless of achievement or status.

Some writers included here—such as Paul Robeson, Carter G. Woodson, John Edgar Wideman, Paul Laurence Dunbar, and Margaret Walker—exhibit no fear of not belonging, cherishing the role of the outsider without any sense of hesitation or ambivalence. The words *submission* or *inferiority* are nowhere to be found in their lexicon. They're not concerned with accep- tance, total assimilation, or being on one's best behavior. Even in writings concerning the black immigrant experience like that in Edwidge Danticat's stirring short-story collection, *Krik? Krak!*, there exists a savvy knowing about the role of the outsider in an America of contradictions, an America of skin color privilege and status quo.

What is celebrated in the words and images of the writers in this section of *Sacred Fire* is individual freedom and the collective power of the alienated, the disinherited, the marginal. These writ- ers wrote to survive, to avoid total assimilation and annihilation, to maintain a power of choice in their daily lives not guaranteed by the ballot box. Style and soul, along with smarts, were essen- tial weaponry in these outsiders' arsenal. These elements of our identity and community were the unique things that set us apart aesthetically from all others, isolated us artistically from Western tradition, separated us spiritually from the American experience.

Yet we always knew who we were, and we spoke up when it was time for us to tell them who we were. Without this wisdom, without this knowledge gained from the many obstacles over- come, we would be a people devoid of strength, a people to be pitied. These writers on the front lines knew that and produced enduring works with this axiom in mind, ever trumpeting the tri- umphs of the past, ever respectful of the steep losses along the way, ever vigilant of the dangers ahead. This section of *Sacred Fire* is an affirmation of their intellectual brilliance, moral cour- age, and spiritual power.

Prize-winning journalist Robert Fleming is the author of The Wis- dom of the Elders.

Lyrics of Lowly Life (1896)

Paul Laurence Dunbar
Poetry

I t is both poignant and ironic that *Lyrics of Lowly Life,* Paul
Laurence Dunbar's third volume of poems and the one to
gain him a national reputation, should also contain the two
poems that would most clearly represent him and reflect the artistic conflict that would torment him throughout his life.

In "We Wear the Mask," the poet speaks of the need to present a false face to the world while suffering inner torment:

> We wear the mask that grins and lies
> It hides our cheeks and shades our eyes,—
> This debt we pay to human guile;
> With torn and bleeding hearts we smile,
> And mouth with myriad subtleties.

And then from "When Malindy Sings":

> G'way and quit that noise, Miss Lucy—
> Put that music book away;
> What's de use to keep on tryn'?
> Ef you practice t'will you'r gray,
> You can't sta't no notes a-flying
> Lak de ones dat rants and rings
> From the kitchen to the big house
> When Malindy sings.

The conflict that tormented Dunbar, one that remained unre-
solved throughout his short life (he died at age thirty-three),
involved his reputation as a poet: While he longed to be taken
seriously and to be acknowledged for his poems in standard English, the racial proscription of the country would allow him
place only for his mastery of "Negro dialect." A good deal of

53

nineteenth-century white America's love of his dialect poetry was based on his benign images of laughing "darkies" and "coons" eatin' and fishin' and dancin' on the plantation.

But in his standard poems, Dunbar showed a more philosophic bent, musing in the Romantic tradition about the natural world and life itself. And while his dialect poems seem to indicate a counterrevolutionary Tom, his standard poems reveal a man with an evolved racial consciousness that, on rare occasions, borders on militance. Poems such as "We Wear the Mask" and "Frederick Douglass" remain sublime testimonies to the difficulties of black life in America. Fortunately, in the century since Dunbar's death, his reputation has come to rightly rest with these and others of his challenging and lyrical standard English poems.

The Conjure Woman (1899)

Charles W. Chestnutt
Novel

C harles W. Chestnutt was the most widely read and influential African American fiction writer of his time and the first ever brought to press by a major publishing house. *The Conjure Woman* introduced the verbal and philosophical richness of African American folk culture to a white readership largely ignorant of true southern black life. Even today, this collection is thought to be among the best representations of life on a southern plantation to be found in American literature.

The Conjure Woman is a collection of "conjuring tales" written in rich dialect. Each of the stories masterfully portrays both the inhumanity of plantation life and the cunning wisdom used by many to survive post–Civil War neoslavery. The stories are more accurate than those written by contemporary writers like Joel Chandler Harris, whose Uncle Remus stories fondly portray life on the plantation. Chestnutt's stories more often reflect the true conditions of plantation life, if in slightly muted tones: forced separation of loved ones, the greed of the slave masters, and the ready violence to be found on the plantations.

Chestnutt's later—and more straightforward—explorations into biracialism, miscegenation, and racisim (*The House Behind the Cedars, The Marrow of Tradition,* and *The Colonel's Dream*) met with so tepid a commercial response that Chestnutt decided to return to his private legal practice in order to support his family. But *The Conjure Woman* has ensured his reputation as a groundbreaking writer of fiction that truthfully tells the stories of slave life.

The Souls of Black Folk (1903)

W. E. B. Du Bois
Nonfiction

"**H**erein lie buried many things, which if read with patience may show the strange meaning of being black here in the dawning of the Twentieth Century."

Born in Massachusetts in 1868, William Edward Burghardt Du Bois was the foremost black intellectual of his time—and mind you, his time stretched all the way from Reconstruction to the civil rights movement of the 1960s. A man of staggering intellect and drive, he was the first black to hold a doctorate from Harvard University. Du Bois wrote three historical works, two novels, two autobiographies, and sixteen pioneering books on sociology, history, politics, and race relations. He was a founder of the NAACP, pioneering Pan-Africanist, spirited advocate for world peace, and tireless fighter for civil rights during the darkest days of Jim Crow.

Du Bois was also a prophet: At the turn of the century, he wrote in the "forethought" of this seminal collection of essays that "the problem of the Twentieth Century is the problem of the color line." That statement has resonated throughout this turbulent century and remains just as fresh today as in 1903. *The Souls of Black Folk,* a collection of fourteen powerfully written essays that are by turn testimony and autobiography, stands as a monumental achievement and quite possibly his most influential work. The book is both a vivid portrait of the conditions facing freshly emancipated black folk at the turn of the century and a still-relevant discussion of the dilemma of race in the United States. It was here that Du Bois introduced his influential concept of "double-consciousness": the struggle of black people trying to define themselves as both black and American.

What makes these unflinching, luminous, and troublesome essays so powerful is that each builds upon the other to try to answer questions about race that have perplexed, enraged, and divided America for over a century. Written in part to counter Booker T. Washington's prevailing strategy of accommodation, *The Souls of Black Folk* created a fresh way of looking at and protesting the multifaceted oppression of black people.

Your country? How came it yours? Before the Pilgrims landed we were here. Here we have brought our three gifts and mingled them with yours: a gift of story and song . . . the gift of sweat and brawn to beat back the wilderness, conquer the soil, and lay the foundations of this vast economic empire two hundred years earlier than your weak hands could have done it; the third, a gift of the Spirit. . . . Are not these gifts worth the giving? Is not this work and striving? Would America have been America without her Negro people?

—from *The Souls of Black Folk*

Cane (1923)

Jean Toomer
Novel

Cane is Jean Toomer's acclaimed exploration of the American racial temperament of the 1920s. Using his own life as a model, Toomer explores the issues of race and identity that simmer just below the fragile American social veneer. Organized in three sections, these stories and vignettes are also interspersed with poetry. Toomer's brilliant interweaving of black folk culture within themes of miscegenation, black sexuality, and racial identity and conflict turned this novel into a literary high point.

Toomer's book represented and served to introduce the now self-aware and emergent "new" Negro. In fact, the author himself was embraced by the white literary avant-garde as a modernist of the first order. While initially a commercial failure, *Cane* is now considered a twentieth-century masterpiece.

Men had always wanted her, this Karintha, even as a child, Karintha carrying beauty, perfect as the dusk when the sun goes down. Old men rode her hobby-horse upon their knees. Young men danced with her at frolics when they should have been dancing with their grown-up girls. God grant us youth, secretly prayed the old men. The young men counted the time to pass before she would be old enough to mate with them. This interest of the male, who wishes to ripen a growing thing too soon, could mean no good to her.

> . . . Her skin is like dusk,
> O can't you see it,
> Her skin is like dusk,
> When the sun goes down.

—from *Cane*

The New Negro (1925)

Alain Locke
Anthology

Alain Locke is the acknowledged Father of the Harlem Renaissance. A highly educated man and the first African American to be awarded a Rhodes scholarship, Locke served as the bridge between a burgeoning literary expression centered in Harlem, New York, and the mainstream literary world. He brought the star writers of the renaissance, including Countee Cullen, Langston Hughes, and Claude McKay, broad literary attention and patrons—wealthy supporters who provided financial support for struggling writers and artists. In this landmark anthology, Locke set forth the defining characteristics of the new Negro who was emerging in America's northern cities: literary, artistic, cosmopolitan, and urbane.

Published in 1925, *The New Negro* is an anthology of poems, stories, and essays edited by Locke that includes such luminaries as W. E. B. Du Bois, James Weldon Johnson, Angelina Grimké, Hughes, Cullen, and McKay. It became a "Who's Who" of the Harlem Renaissance and its defining text. Like the renaissance itself, *The New Negro* was a symbol of the literary fruit of the great migration of blacks from the rural South to the urban North. Locke was sure that Harlem was fast becoming a new mecca of black artistry and one of the world's cultural capitals, an assertion that was not hard to argue on the basis of the outstanding work represented in this volume.

The best of the work created during the renaissance—the criticism of Du Bois, the poetry of Johnson and Hughes, the fiction of McKay—has endured. And the Harlem of the 1920s and 1930s remains one of the iconic places in African American history: full of jazz, creativity, and beautiful black people on the move. But what became of the new Negro, that artful and cosmopolitan urbanite? There were lofty expectations, to be sure, but in retrospect and beyond the stardust, the Harlem Renaissance presented to the new Negro a hard lesson: the real work of the culture lay in assuring its permanence, not just basking in the flow of transient praise and voguishness. The artists of the renaissance were heavily dependent on the patronage of their fellow New Yorkers downtown, and Harlem's renaissance died out with onset of the Great Depression, when the patronage stopped flowing in even as Harlem's most enduring artists continued to produce important work. Nevertheless, the spirit of the so-called new Negro, the spirit of vital black urban creativity embodied in the works found in this collection, lives on.

In Harlem, Negro life is seizing upon its first chances for group expression and self-determination. It is—or promises at least to be—a race capital. That is why our comparison is taken with those nascent centers of folk-expression and self-determination which are playing a creative part in the world today. Without pretense to their political significance, Harlem has the same role to play for the New Negro as Dublin has had for the New Ireland or Prague for the New Czechoslovakia.

—from *The New Negro*

The Blacker the Berry (1929)

Wallace Thurman
Novel

Wallace Thurman's brilliantly sly novel *The Blacker the Berry* is about skin color, blackness, and the color bias of "golden browns," "mulattos," "high yallers," and "nearly whites" against the "dark browns," "blue-blacks," and "Hottentots."

This is the tragic tale of Emma Lou Brown, a very dark sister whose indigo complexion gives her endless grief and humiliation at the hands of her lighter-complected family. Emma Lou's relatives "couldn't stomach" black people. After years of being the darkest spot of color in her near-white black family, Emma escapes to Harlem, hoping to fit in or at least to disappear. "More acutely than ever before Emma Lou began to feel that her luscious black complexion was somewhat of a liability, and that her marked color variation from the other people in her environment was a curse. Not that she minded being black, being a Negro necessitated having a colored skin, but she did mind being too black. . . . Why had her mother married a black man? Surely there had been some eligible brown-skin men around."

The Blacker the Berry is clever, beautifully written, sharp, and searing. Emma is every black woman who has ever been told to wear a hat for fear of getting any darker, who has cursed her African features, or who has been told to choose a lighter mate to lighten her offspring. Every line, word, and phrase in Thurman's bitter masterpiece is pure truth; therein lies its power.

The Mis-education of the Negro
(1933, latest rev. ed., 1969)

Carter G. Woodson
History

C arter G. Woodson has been called the Father of Modern Black History. He was a central, commanding figure in the study, writing, and teaching of African American history and the first historian to successfully use sound scholarship to refute the prevailing myths and racist views about black Americans and their history. Among his contributions to American life is Black History Month (originally dubbed Negro History Week), which Woodson established to promote the study of African American history.

Woodson's 205-page monograph, *The Mis-education of the Negro,* reflects his profound concern for setting the record straight. His thesis, as outlined in his Preface, could well apply today: "The so-called modern education, with all its defects, however, does others so much more good than it does the Negro, because it has been worked out in conformity to the needs of those who have enslaved and oppressed weaker people." He was concerned with the way African American identity had been warped by racist approaches to history and education; he foresaw the ways that such a warped history would be internalized by black students who would never know of the achievements of their forebears, only of their humiliations and sufferings.

In the book's eighteen chapters, Woodson presents a systematic critique of the education system and offers a plan for change that would create a system that informs black students about their own history and addresses their unique challenges. The current proliferation of African American studies programs, Afro-centric schools, and multicultural curricula all bear Woodson's stamp. Still, *Mis-education* remains a biting indictment of a public school system whose promise of education of the masses has still been left sadly unfulfilled.

The Ways of White Folks (1934)

Langston Hughes
Short Stories

If you are not yet familiar with Langston Hughes, then his collection *The Ways of White Folks* (named in homage to Du Bois's classic *The Souls of Black Folk*) is the perfect introduction to his mordant wit and unerring eye for detail and his sly and direct prose.

These stories move from poignant to funny, to seething with rage, often within a paragraph. And life, as it is painted here, is bleak and unchanging until death. Hughes's characters inhabit a world where people are mean because they can be, and where hard work is all that is guaranteed; these were the harsh realities for blacks in America in the twenties and thirties. If, as Du Bois contended in his book, "the problem of the twentieth century is the problem of the color line," this collection allows Hughes to illustrate that point time and again. He demonstrates to white readers what he and his black readers knew: "White folks is white folks, South or North, North or South." This is the concept he used to structure his seemingly mundane yet tragic tales.

"Cora Unashamed" reveals how lifelong servitude can render the servant almost invisible, even to herself. In "Passing," a mixed-race black passes for white, forever denying his race and family: "I felt like a dog, passing you downtown last night and not speaking to you. You were great, though, didn't give a sign that you even knew me, let alone that I was your son."

From North to South, light to dark, prosperous to dirt poor, all the stories are bound together and made powerful by the fact that they were all regular occurrences at that time in the United

States. Within his simple stories, Hughes offered a barbed and trenchant analysis of white behavior and black behavior. Like his poems, the cruel accuracy of *The Ways of White Folks* is a reminder to Americans of some hard truths about the ridiculous and tragic ways skin color warps our lives.

Black Boy (1945)

Richard Wright
Memoir

> *[Wright] came like a sledgehammer, like a giant out of the*
> *mountain with a sledgehammer, writing with a sledgehammer . . .*
>
> —John Henrik Clarke

B *lack Boy* is Richard Wright's unforgettable story of growing up in the Jim Crow South. Published in 1945, it is often considered a fictionalized autobiography or an autobiographical novel because of Wright's use of fiction techniques (and possibly fictional events) to tell his story. Nevertheless, the book is a lyrical and skillfully wrought description of Wright's hungry youth in rural Mississippi and Memphis, told from the perspective of the adult Wright, who was still trying to come to grips with the cruel deprivations and humiliations of his childhood.

Life in the pre–civil rights South was intensely alienating for young Richard. At every turn, his desire to communicate was stunted, whether by family members who insisted he "hush!" or by teachers who harassed and mocked him. He was surrounded by people he considered contemptibly ignorant, people who willingly allowed their lives to be restricted by tradition and authority no matter how illegitimate or self-destructive. Whether they were racist whites or passive, uncompassionate blacks, his fellow southerners viewed Richard's independence and intelligence with suspicion and scorned and humiliated him for his family's poverty. He lashed out by hitting the streets: He was already drinking by the time he turned six, and he fought constantly. He finally found his outlet in writing; by the end of the book, he decided that there was nothing he could ever do to improve his life in the South and committed to moving to Chicago to pursue his art.

When first published, *Black Boy* was considered by many to be an angry attack on the racist South because of Wright's hard-hitting portrayal of the racism he faced, not to mention his already-acquired reputation as a "protest writer." But the book's value goes deeper than that: Wright bears witness to the American struggle for the right of self-definition. His own quest to escape the suffocating world of his childhood and find a place where he could freely exercise his individuality, creativity, and integrity was ultimately successful. But *Black Boy* also offers insight into an entire culture of people, both black and white, who had unthinkingly accepted a narrowly prescribed course of life. As Wright put it, "[though] they lived in America where in theory there existed equality of opportunity, they knew unerringly what to aspire to and what not to aspire to." Despite Wright's stifling environment, his story is inspirational for its portrait of how a black boy shucked off the limited expectations of those around him and dared to aspire.

Black Metropolis: A Study of Negro Life in a Northern City (1945)

St. Clair Drake and Horace Cayton
Nonfiction

The cry "Up North!" and the city of Chicago became syn-onymous as America's second city absorbed the masses during the great black migration of 1910 to 1940. This great migration was a watershed event in American history, trans-forming the lives of millions of black people and the cities to which they flocked. It had the obvious outcome of turning a primarily southern, rural people into one identified, for bet-ter or worse, with the inner cities of the American North and West.

Originally published in 1945, the award-winning, two-volume *Black Metropolis* is the work of two eminent social scientists, anthro-pologist St. Clair Drake and sociologist Horace Cayton, trying to describe what this massive movement of people had wrought. It takes as its subject for study one of the largest black communities in the world, at the time, Chicago's inner city, nicknamed Bronze-ville. Richard Wright wrote the preface to the 1945 edition. In it he said:

> Chicago is the city from which the most incisive and radical Negro thought has come; there is an open and raw beauty about that city that seems to either kill or endow one with the spirit of life. I felt those extremes of possibility, death and hope, while I lived half hungry and afraid in a city to which I had fled . . . it was not until I stumbled upon science that I discovered some of the meaning of the environment that battered and taunted me. . . . *Black Metropolis,* Drake's and Cayton's scien-

tific statement about the urban Negro, pictures the environment out of which the Bigger Thomases of our nation come.

This study is critical in locating the site and tracing the circumstances under which southern dreams of freedom and prosperity up North were dashed. It is critical to understanding the modern history of the disenfranchisement of the African American.

Invisible Man (1952)

Ralph Ellison
Novel

*I*nvisible Man—incredibly, Ralph Ellison's first and only novel—is one of the lasting masterpieces of American literature. It chronicles the existential journey of an unnamed black man attempting to discover his identity and role in a hostile and confusing world that refuses to acknowledge his existence.

Within the story of the protagonist's quest for definition, Ellison offers a vivid and unforgiving examination of the shortcomings of the self-serving black bourgeoisie, clumsy white philanthropists, dehumanizing American industry, and unrealistic revolutionary movements. The narrator jointly tells his own, personal coming-of-age story—one that takes him from the deep South to the streets of Harlem, from workaday jobs to revolution, from a black college to (literally) a hole in the ground—and the symbolic story of the unfinished coming of age of his race in America. Ellison skillfully manages to tell both stories without ever reducing his narrator to a flat symbol of everyblackman, allowing the story to work successfully on both levels.

The novel also benefits from Ellison's rich narrative style, which drew from a heady mix of influences. He incorporated the jazzy rhythms and vivid imagery of black American speech, music, and folklore in his tale, while also showing the influence of white writers such as Melville, Twain, and Dostoyevsky.

Invisible Man is an essential book, whether read as an intriguing coming-of-age story, an incisive portrait of an individual's quest for identity, or a powerful indictment of the absurdity of racism that remains fresh and relevant today. Ellison's stylish prose speaks to the individual and collective need to acquire self-knowledge, self-definition, self-illumination—to become visible to ourselves.

I am not a spook like those who haunted Edgar Allan Poe; nor am I one of your Hollywood-movie ectoplasms. I am a man of substance, of flesh and bone, fiber and liquids—and I might even be said to possess a mind. I am invisible, understand, simply because people refuse to see me. Like the bodiless heads you see sometimes in circus sideshows, it is as though I have been surrounded by mirrors of hard, distorted glass. When they approach me they see only my surroundings, themselves, or figments of their imagination—indeed, everything and anything except me.

—from the Prologue to *Invisible Man*

Go Tell It on the Mountain (1953)

James Baldwin
Novel

*G*o *Tell It on the Mountain* is considered to be James Baldwin's greatest novel. Like much of Baldwin's writing, it draws heavily on his own intense childhood experiences with religious doubt, racism, sexual ambivalence, and a complex relationship with a difficult father. The entire book takes place on the fourteenth birthday of John Grimes, the son of a fire-and-brimstone revivalist preacher, who finds himself increasingly alienated from his bitter, authoritarian father, his religious faith, and his community. Baldwin treats the young man's battle with Manichaean choices—flesh or spirit, community or individualism, conversion or heresy—with masterful sensitivity and insight.

The book is divided into three parts: In part one, we share John's terror as he becomes aware that his desires and goals lie outside of the narrow expectations of his family and community. In the second part, we learn of the sorrowful experiences back South and up North that forever scarred John's father, Gabriel, and his mother, Elizabeth, even though they hoped their union would wash away the sins of their past. In part three, John surrenders himself to religious ecstasy, still seeking a way out of his dilemma.

Go Tell It on the Mountain is filled with biblical references that evoke the spirit of the black church and a realism that brings to life the Harlem of the 1930s, a northern ghetto whose inhabitants were still struggling with southern demons. Baldwin, in a 1984 interview with the *Paris Review,* captured what he was trying to say in the novel about all of us and about his own life: "[Writing *Go Tell It on the Mountain*] was an attempt to exorcise something, to find out what happened to my father, what happened to all of us, what had happened to me and how we were to move from one place to another." Its brilliant style and sophisticated portrait of a young man struggling with complex issues made this one of the landmark novels of the postwar period.

Things Fall Apart (1958)

Chinua Achebe
Novel

*T*hings Fall Apart is one of the most widely read African novels ever published. It is written by one of Nigeria's leading novelists, Chinua Achebe. Set in the Ibo village of Umuofia, *Things Fall Apart* recounts a stunning moment in African history—its colonization by Britain. The novel, first published in 1958, has by today sold over 8 million copies, been translated into at least forty-five languages, and earned Achebe the somewhat misleading and patronizing title of "the man who invented African literature." It carefully re-creates tribal life before the arrival of Europeans in Africa, and then details the jarring changes brought on by the advent of colonialism and Christianity.

The book is a parable that examines the colonial experience from an African perspective, through Okonkwo, who was "a strong individual and an Igbo hero struggling to maintain the cultural integrity of his people against the overwhelming power of colonial rule." Okonkwo is banished from the community for accidentally killing a clansman and is forced to live seven years in exile. He returns to his home village, only to witness its disintegration as it abandons tradition for European ways. The book describes the simultaneous disintegration of Okonkwo and his village, as his pleas to his people not to exchange their culture for that of the English fall on deaf ears.

The brilliance of *Things Fall Apart* is that it addresses the imposition of colonization and the crisis in African culture caused by the collapse of colonial rule. Achebe prophetically argued that colonial domination and the culture it left in Africa had such a stranglehold on African peoples that its consequences would haunt African society long after colonizers had left the continent.

The arrival of the missionaries had caused a considerable stir. There were six of them and one was a white man. The white man began to speak to them through an interpreter who was an Ibo man, though his dialect was different and harsh to the ears, but who said he was one of them, as they could see from his color and his language. "We have been sent by God to ask you to leave your wicked ways and false gods," he told them.

—from *Things Fall Apart*

A Raisin in the Sun (1959)

Lorraine Hansberry
Play

A Raisin in the Sun, written by the then twenty-nine-year-old Hansberry, was the "movin' on up" morality play of the 1960s. Martin had mesmerized millions, and integration was seen as the stairway to heaven. *Raisin* had something for everyone, and for this reason it was the recipient of the prestigious New York Drama Critics Circle Award.

The place: a tenement flat in Southside, Chicago. The time: post–World War II. Lena Younger, the strong-willed matriarch, is the glue that holds together the Younger family. Walter Lee is her married, thirty-something son who, along with his wife and sister, lives in his mother's apartment. He is short on meeting responsibilities but long on dreams. Beneatha (that's right, Beneatha) is Walter's sister—an upwardly mobile college student who plans to attend medical school.

Mama Lena is due a check from her late husband's insurance, and Walter Lee is ready to invest it in a liquor store. The money represents his opportunity to assert his manhood. It will bring the jump start he needs to set his life right. Beneatha tells him that it's "mama's money to do with as she pleases," and that she doesn't really expect any for her schooling. However, Mama wants to use her new money for a new beginning—in a new house, in a new neighborhood (white).

Walter cries, and Mama relents. She refrains from paying cash for the house and places a deposit instead, giving Walter the difference to share equally between his investment and Beneatha's college fund. Walter squanders the entire amount. Meanwhile, Mama receives a call from the neighborhood "welcome committee" hoping to dissuade the family from moving in.

While roundly criticized for being politically accommodating to whites, *Raisin* accurately reflected the aspirations of a newly nascent black middle class.

Blues People: Negro Music in White America (1963)

LeRoi Jones
Criticism

D uring the early 1960s as the civil rights movement was gain-
ing intensity, American society—particularly its young—
was also experiencing an upheaval. One of its many reflections
was a new interest in black music, especially the blues: Social and
political countercurrents of the era led many of the sixties generation to embrace the blues as an honest, direct, and earthy
people's alternative to establishment culture. Contemporaneous
with that movement, in 1963 poet/playwright LeRoi Jones (now
Amiri Baraka) published a collection of essays that has since
become pivotal to any discussion of African American music and
culture: "*Blues People*," commented *Library Journal* at the time,
"is American musical history; it is also American culture, economic, and even emotional history. It traces not only the development of the Negro music which affected white America, but
also the Negro values which affected America."

Blues People takes the major African American contributions
to American music—jazz, the blues, spirituals, and rock and
roll—and describes them in the context of the wider story of
African American history and culture. Jones carefully draws out
the connections between the social and political frustrations of
black folks in America and their incredible musical expressiveness
and invention. He identifies the source of this musical genius as
the "blues impulse" and traces its evolution from the spirituals
and work songs of enslaved Africans to the twentieth-century
explosions of blues, jazz, and rock and roll.

This is far from a dry sociological study; Baraka infuses his
discussion with his obvious love of the subject and writes with the

same sharp intelligence, insight, and playful wit that he brings to his poetry, drama, and prose. This book provides a crucial understanding of the dark and difficult wellsprings of African American popular music.

The Negro slave is one thing. The Negro as American is quite another. But the path the slave took to "citizenship" is what I want to look at. And I make my analogy through the slave citizen's music—through the music that is closely associated with him: blues and a later, but parallel development, jazz. And it seems to me that if the Negro represents, or is symbolic of, something in and about the nature of American culture, this certainly should be revealed by his characteristic music.

—from *Blues People*

Jubilee (1966)

Margaret Walker

Novel

W hen Margaret Walker's grandmother used to tell her stories about her mother's life as a slave on a southern
plantation, Walker vowed that she would one day share those stories with the world. *Jubilee* is not only the fictional recounting of
Dr. Walker's great-grandmother's life, it is also a black woman's
view of the political, economic, and social structure of the plantation system before the Civil War—a powerful response to the
gilded images of plantation life found in novels such as *Gone with
the Wind*. Through the story of Vyry Brown, a fierce and fearless
black woman, daughter of a slave and a slave owner, *Jubilee*
focuses on the sounds and textures of everyday life on a plantation for a black woman. It is also among the first books to
describe the tricky relationship between black women and white
women, a relationship whose intimate roots in slavery are dis-
cussed here.

The novel is divided into three sections: The first, "Sis
Hetta's Child—the Ante-Bellum Years," covers Vyry's childhood
and first encounters with the sorrows of love under the slave system. It ends with a failed escape attempt. The second section,
"My Eyes Have Seen the Glory," examines Vyry's life as a nurse
during the Civil War. The final section, "Forty Years in the
Wilderness—Reconstruction and Reaction," covers the period
after emancipation, when Vyry and her family face new trou-
bles—natural disasters, the Ku Klux Klan, and the abounding
racism of the South after the Civil War. In every phase of life,
Vyry meets her challenges with grit, intelligence, grace, and
strength.

Jubilee was lauded for its warm, engaging prose and its authenticity. In fact, it took Walker thirty years to research and write the book. The research shows itself in the way she is able to re-create the most intimate details of Vyry's life—her everyday routine, the language she used, the foods she ate, her pastimes and passions. The book is also noteworthy for its presentation of a heroic African American woman born in slavery. It is astounding that anyone could think that black women survived the abuse and exploitation of slavery without immense reserves of strength, wits, and courage, but America had chosen happy, hysterical, and mindless mammies and pickaninnies as the popular image of antebellum black womanhood. Smart, tough Vyry was a wonderful correction to those stereotypes. First published in 1966, the book's first edition went through nineteen printings.

Black Skin, White Masks (1967)

Frantz Fanon
Nonfiction

T hat the writing of the Martinique-born psychiatrist, intellectual, and revolutionary Frantz Fanon should become
seminal to African Americans during the tumultuous black power
period is not surprising. As biographer Peter Geismar has written:

> Fanon's writings were first fully appreciated within the Western
> civilization that he attacked so violently: His books have
> become required reading for the black revolutionaries in the
> United States who consider their people as part of the Third
> World—a term commonly used to designate the whole of the
> undeveloped world.

The accuracy of Fanon's analysis of the psychological situation of
the oppressed arose from firsthand experience, from his own early
encounter with Western civilization during his student days in
France. He has recorded that encounter in his first book, *Black
Skin, White Masks* (originally published in 1952). Through a systematic psychological analysis, Fanon attempts to articulate (and
perhaps to also exorcise) the psychic trauma of the colonized.

Published in America in 1967, *Black Skin, White Masks* inves-
tigates "the warping of the Negro psyche by a 'superior' white
culture." Fanon describes his reasons for writing the book as follows: "My consciousness is not illuminated with ultimate radi-
ances. Nevertheless . . . I think it would be good if certain things
were said. These things I am going to say, not shout. For it is a
long time since shouting has gone out of my life . . . Why write
this book? . . . I reply quite calmly that there are too many idiots
in this world. And having said it, I have the burden of proving it."

And he does. In his inimitable straightforward style, Fanon pokes fun, but in all seriousness, at what he saw as empty rhetoric regarding relationships between blacks and whites. If you have not yet read Fanon, start here with his first book, which is filled with his sharp observances and piercing humor. "This book should have been written three years ago . . . but these truths were fire in me then. Now I can tell them without being burned. These truths are not intended to be hurled in men's faces. They are not intended to ignite fervor. I do not trust fervor."

Even if you do not appreciate Fanon's arguments, you will be struck by the clarity of his tone and the magnitude of his vision.

The Crisis of the Negro Intellectual
(1967)

Harold Cruse
Nonfiction

H arold Cruse's *The Crisis of the Negro Intellectual* was one of the most controversial and influential books written during the late 1960s Black Power period. In it, Cruse makes a spirited, polemical argument about the failure of the black bourgeoisie, artists, and intellectuals to create autonomous black cultural institutions and scholarship and criticizes their dependence on white institutions and ideologies. The book landed like a bomb in academic and cultural circles, and its influence continues to be felt today.

Cruse traced the recent history of African American intellectual life to highlight the patterns of failure at each juncture. The Harlem Renaissance, a much-vaunted flowering of black intellectual and artistic life, failed because its leaders allowed, and even encouraged, white patronage to be its lifeblood. Black intellectuals in subsequent decades allowed themselves to be controlled by communists, who while encouraging blacks to integrate with them, maintained their own ethnic institutions. Cruse argued that black intellectuals who failed to create a paradigm for looking at the world based on black sensibilities and viewpoints were abdicating their responsibility to their less-educated brothers and sisters. By allowing ostensibly sympathetic white intellectuals to frame the American discussion of race, these black intellectuals removed themselves, and their constituency by extension, from that vital debate.

Cruse's book has had wide-reaching ramifications in black scholarship since its publication. It has been criticized by scholars across the ideological spectrum, including Afrocentrists, whom Cruse derided as "ceremonial nationalists." But whether they agreed or disagreed, his powerful and impassioned plea for a black cultural nationalism influenced a generation of intellectuals to reassess the relevance of their work.

We a BaddDDD People (1970)

Sonia Sanchez

Poetry

S onia Sanchez is one of the most admired and enduring poets to come out of the Black Arts Movement in the late 1960s and early 1970s. *We a BaddDDD People* is a classic from that period, a collection of poems that spoke to the revolutionary yearnings of the black masses in their native tongue. The revolution she espoused was one of self-love and self-knowledge in the face of racist hate; the African rhythms she created in her poetry (especially when she read it aloud) and her use of black vernacular were poetic manifestations of that drive toward communal self-love.

Characterizing Sanchez's poetry of that period, critic Gloria Wade-Gayles says,

> [Sanchez] used the language of the people rather than the polished language of the academy, mixing images of the ghetto, lower-case letters, dashes, slashes, hyphenated lines, abbreviations, unorthodox spelling, and other experiments with language and form to redefine what a poem is, what it does, and for whom it is written.

As Sanchez herself explains it, "I see myself helping to bring forth the truth about the world. I cannot tell the truth about anything unless I confess to being a student, growing and learning something new everyday. The more I learn, the clearer my view of the world becomes. To gain that clarity . . . I had to wash my ego in the needs/aspirations of my people." *We a BaddDDD People* is a lyrical tribute to the revolutionary aspiration of black people to discover and love themselves despite the hostility of the world around them.

The Hero and the Blues (1973)

Albert Murray
Nonfiction

According to Murray in *The Hero and the Blues*, in literature "storybook images are indispensable to the basic human processes of world comprehension and self-definition. . . . the most delicately wrought short stories and the most elaborately textured novels, along with the homespun anecdotes, parables, fables, tales, legends, and sagas, are as strongly motivated by immediate educational objectives as are signs, labels . . . and directives. . . . To make the telling more effective is to make the tale more to the point, more meaningful, and in consequence, if not coincidentally, more useful. Nor is the painter or the musician any less concerned than the writer with achieving a telling effect."

So begins Murray's three-part essay to writers, editors, educators, publishers, reviewers, and teachers, scolding them for having forgotten that "fiction of its very nature is most germane and useful not when it restricts itself to . . . social and political agitation and propaganda . . . but when it performs the fundamental and universal functions of literature." Murray, an academician and historian, believed that literature established the context for social and political action. And that the writer, who created stories or narrated incidents that embodied aspects of human nature, not only described them but also suggested possibilities that could contribute most to people's welfare.

Calling on Dostoyevsky, Hemingway, Thomas Mann, Marx, Freud, Malcolm X, Eldridge Cleaver, Count Basie, Duke Ellington, and many others to support his premise, Murray's slim but sweeping narrative praises the artist, writer, and musician as social commentator and educator, as long as he doesn't venture far from his storytelling roots.

Song of Solomon (1977)

Toni Morrison
Novel

S ong of Solomon, Toni Morrison's lyrical third novel, begins
with an arresting scene—a man on a roof threatening to
jump, a woman standing on the ground, singing, and another
woman entering labor. The child born of that labor is Macon
"Milkman" Dead III; *Song of Solomon* is the epic story of his lifetime journey toward an understanding of his own identity and
ancestry. Milkman is born burdened with the materialistic values
of his father and the weight of a racist society; over the course of
his odyssey he reconnects to his deeper family values and history,
rids himself of the burden of his father's expectations and society's limitations, and literally learns to fly.

When the novel opens, Milkman is clearly a man with little or
no concern for others. Like his father, he is driven only by his
immediate sensual needs; he is spoiled and self-centered and pur-
sues money and sexual gratification at all costs. The novel centers
around his search for a lost bag of gold that was allegedly taken
from a man involved in his grandfather's murder and then abandoned by his Aunt Pilate. The search for gold takes Milkman and
his friend Guitar, a young black militant, to Shalimar, a town
named for his great-grandfather Solomon, who according to local
legend escaped slavery by taking flight back to Africa on the wind.
On his journey, under the influence of his Aunt Pilate, a strong,
fearless, natural woman whose values are the opposite of Milkman's father's, Milkman begins to come to terms with his family
history, his role as a man, and the possibilities of his life apart
from a cycle of physical lust and satisfaction.

In telling the story of Milkman's quest to discover the hidden
history of the Deads, Morrison expertly weaves together elements

As fleet and bright as a lodestar he wheeled toward Guitar and it did not matter which of them would give up his ghost in the killing arms of his brother. For now he knew what Shalimar knew: If you surrendered to the air, you could *ride* it.

—from *Song of Solomon*

of myth, magic, and folklore. She grapples with fundamental issues of class and race, ancestry and identity, while never losing sight of Milkman's compelling story. The language in *Song of Solomon,* Morrison's only novel with a male protagonist, is earthy and poetic, the characters eccentric, and the detail vivid and convincing. The result is a novel that is at once emotionally intense, provocative, and inspiring in its description of how one man rediscovered the latent power within him.

Song of Solomon is considered to be Toni Morrison's masterpiece and is in the top echelon of literary works produced by any American writer. It is also her breakthrough novel in both critical and commercial success: It was the first African American novel since *Native Son* to be a main selection of the Book of the Month club and it won the prestigious National Book Critics Circle Award among others. The book received a second life, and bestseller status, twenty years after its initial publication when talk show host Oprah Winfrey announced it as a selection for her on-air book club.

Elbow Room (1981)

James Alan McPherson
Short Stories

James Alan McPherson is one of the best American short
story writers to come out of the 1960s and 1970s. His first
volume of short stories, *Hue and Cry,* was published in the same
year he graduated from Harvard Law School at the age of 25. His
second collection, *Elbow Room,* won him the Pulitzer Prize for
fiction in 1981.

McPherson's prime gift as a writer is his ability to draw utterly
believable, and sympathetic, characters. The men and women
brought to life in the stories of *Elbow Room* are folks you already
know from the barbershops, trains, and backrooms of black communities North and South. Their words are easy to recognize,
and their situations all too familiar. But the familiarity we feel
with the characters only heightens the sense of melancholy that
pervades these stories. The stories center around the differences
between people—differences in race, outlook, beliefs—that more
often than not prove to be irreconcilable. Sometimes, those differences are treated to gently comic effect, as in the poignant
remembrances of "Why I Love Square Dancing." Other times,
the stories evoke rousing black folktales of "bad men," as in "The
Story of a Dead Man." And sometimes McPherson, in spite of
himself, offers hope, as in the title story, whose main character,
Virginia, makes "elbow room" in her head for the differences
among people.

This collection offers a wide range of compelling writing,
finely drawn characters, and provocative situations. Even when
McPherson's stories center on relations between the races, his
characters express universal truths about humanity and how we
interact in the spaces we share.

Damballah (1984)

John Edgar Wideman
Novel

John Edgar Wideman grew up in the Homewood section of
Pittsburgh, a setting he has used for a number of his award-
winning novels and stories. *Damballah,* Wideman's collection of
stories about the fictionalized black community of Homewood, is
the first in a trilogy consisting of *Damballah, Hiding Place,* and
Sent for You Yesterday. Somewhat autobiographical, the books are
linked by shared characters, events, and locales. Like much of
Wideman's writing, the stories in *Damballah* are intense and lyrical examinations of the intense psychological experience of black
people in urban America.

The first story, "Orion," is about an African brought to
an American plantation who wants to teach "the old ways"
to a young slave. Knowing that only in death can he do so,
he sets out to get it. "One scream that night. Like a bull when
they cut off his maleness. . . . A bull screaming once that
night and torches burning in the barn and Master and the
men coming out and no Ryan. . . Mistress crying behind
a locked door and Master messing with Patty down the
quarters."

"Hazel" is the story of a young girl accidentally crippled by
her brother and who is now trapped by her mother's good inten-
tions. "When I look at you sitting in that chair . . . I can't tell you
what a trial it is. Then I think . . . there's a whole lot she'll never
have to suffer. . . . The lies of men, their nasty hands . . . having
their way, having their babies."

Wideman's writing is powerfully visceral, not tempered with
sentiment or poetic prose, which is one reason it is not more

widely read than it is. His intelligent and inventive use of language and his concern with the psychological issues that affect African Americans, however, make his work essential. *Damballah* is pure Wideman, and if you have not yet read him, it is a good place to start.

A Hard Road to Glory: A History of the African American Athlete (1993: Vol. 1, 1619 to 1918; Vol. 2, 1919 to 1945; Vol. 3, Since 1946)

Arthur Ashe
Nonfiction

A Hard Road to Glory is, in three volumes, the definitive history of black athletics in America. A work of monumental importance to African American history, it traces the development of African American athletes from Africa in the seventeenth century to today. The book took Ashe over six years to compile, requiring the assistance of a professional research staff and the advice of several world-famous scholars. So committed was Ashe to this project that the majority of the staggering costs of research came out of his own pocket. The book that was ultimately produced puts the iconic image of the African American athlete back into the context of black cultural and social life over the centuries.

"The 1920s was known as the 'Golden Decade of Sports' . . . Of course it should have been more appropriately called 'The Golden Decade of (White) Sports,' for black athletes were shut out of major league baseball, eased out of professional football, not allowed to join a fledgling professional basketball league, barred from Forest Hills in tennis, and unlawfully kept out of contention for the heavyweight boxing crown."

Ashe thought that by drawing attention to the historical barring of blacks from the opportunities available through professional sports, he could help aspiring black sports enthusiasts. "Today, thousands of young African Americans continue to seek their places in the sun through athletics. . . . Perhaps this history will ease the journey with sober reflections of how difficult and improbable the hard road really is."

In his twenty-year tennis career, Ashe won some of the most coveted tennis championships in the game. An eloquent statesman and gifted writer, he was also the author of *Off the Court* and *Days of Grace*.

Krik? Krak! (1995)

Edwidge Danticat
Short Stories

W hen Haitian storytellers get ready to tell a story, they say *"Krik?"* Their eager listeners respond, *"Krak!"* With *Krik? Krak!* Edwidge Danticat established herself as a superior storyteller within and without Haiti's narrative tradition. *Krik? Krak!* reveals the wonder, terror, and pain of Danticat's native Haiti and the enduring strength of Haitian women. Danticat writes about the terrorism of the Tonton Macoutes; the death of hope and the resiliency of love; the Haitians who fled to America to give their children a better life, as her parents did; and the bridge to the past through the tradition of storytelling.

The first seven stories are about chaotic life under political oppression and poverty in Haiti, and the imaginative strategies devised by Haitians to maintain their ideals and hopes in the face of unfathomable hardship. The powerful first story, "Children of the Sea," sets the tone for the Haitian stories. It is a moving series of diary entries from alternating narrators: a young man fleeing Haiti on a dilapidated boat and his girlfriend back on the island, who is living in fear of her life and of his. The last two stories, based in New York City, demonstrate how even after leaving their homeland, Danticat's Haitian characters cling to their heritage while trying to adapt to a new land and a new set of opportunities.

The stories are about people who embrace mythic powers and rites of passage and people who long for peace and happiness for themselves and their country. Danticat captured readers and reviewers with her passion and lyrical writing in what she refers to as her distant third language. A finalist for the National Book Award and Danticat's second book, *Krik? Krak!* is full of vibrant imagery and grace that bear witness to the Haitian people's suffering and courage.

Politics, Nationalism, and Revolution

Commentary

by Arthur Flowers

The Destruction of Black Civilization made me cry. Sure did. I had just read it, back in the 70s I think, and was biking down 125th Street thinking about how far we've traveled and how far we've fallen and was suddenly just crying, vowing never again. I'll never forget that moment. Encounters with books are as responsible as anything for my own still-evolving understanding and lifelong commitment to the struggle.

Works of struggle have pride of place in black literature. A culture's literature is that culture's communal voice. As such, the literature inevitably reflects the traumas that culture is going through at any given time, its burning survival issues. Since the beginning of our journey in the West, it can be argued that the Struggle has been a primary trope of black people in America and around the modern world. Which way freedom? Black literature has consistently reflected the ongoing struggle for survival and empowerment waged by the black people of America and the world. It would be difficult to overestimate the importance of the revolutionary impulse in black literature.

The earliest of our literature, the slave narratives, struggled with the critical questions of the time—freedom and slavery, assimilation and resistance. With the transformation of black America from a rural peasantry to an urban people during the great migration, the burning questions became those of urbanization and cultural survival in an increasingly complex society. The Black Arts Movement, along with the concurrent civil rights and Black Power movements, was fundamentally concerned with issues of identity and empowerment. It was during this period that the literature, and black America as a whole, turned its primary energies from protest addressed to white audiences to a more internal focus. A healing thing.

The literature reflects back to us who we are and passes the word on to future generations. It is a primary tool of cultural retention and orchestration, of the process by which a culture selects the trends and impulses it decides are pertinent to its survival and prosperity. It is the literature that records and defines ideas and values, that forges the visions by which we live and strive, by which we dream. Literature opens minds and passes on ideas, allowing folks to see themselves and their lives in new perspectives, what Julie Dash calls "rupturing their reality."

Marcus Garvey was highly influenced by the book *Ethiopia Unbound* by Casely Hayford, from which he took, among others, the phrase "One God, One People, One Destiny." In turn, Marcus Garvey influenced not only thousands and thousands of black folks, he also influenced the historical dynamics of his times and therefore the future. It can be argued that he has influenced millions of black folks through his writings in *Africa for the Africans*. This happens to some degree every time a reader is touched by a work.

As the voices of a culture that has from its inception felt itself under mortal siege, black people in America and around the world have always valued the voices of struggle. This is, in part, a cultural legacy. The griotic impulse is strong in our literature. Africa's oral tradition and art have been both sacred and functional. Black literature is working literature, and black writers have never been afraid to speak truth to power.

There is something endearing about the willingness of black writers to speak when called, no matter the cost. Martin Luther King had to speak up for his movement, even from the cold floor of a jail cell in *Letter from a Birmingham Jail*. David Walker wrote his *Appeal* and was soon after found dead in the streets of Boston. And what was on the mind of Malcolm when he knew criticism of the Nation, as found in his posthumous *Autobiography of Malcolm X*, could cost him his life. Or on the minds of slaves like Frederick Douglass, who risked torture and death to learn how to read and write, who instinctively understood that the word was a magic that would literally free them from bondage?

Why do tyrants quake when writers speak? Because the Word means something. Because the people trust true writers to care for them and to speak when they need a voice, because the world listens when writers of conscience speak.

That's why Wole Soyinka had to flee Nigeria in the dead of the night for daring to say the generals had no clothes. At least he got away; his fellow writer Ken Saro Wiwa didn't. "If they treat me like this with my international rep," said Saro Wiwa at his show trial, "imagine how they treat those who have no voice." He left last words before they hanged him: "I give my soul to God, but the struggle continues."

The Struggle. It is the Struggle that shapes us, it is the Struggle we must shape. These works of struggle are works that are essential reading for those who aspire to be truly self-determinant in an increasingly complex world that severely marginalizes the unsophisticated and the uninformed. They are essential reading for those who care about the destiny of our people. They are shield and spear.

Today, our problems seem sometimes insurmountable. But they have always seemed insurmountable. Slavery, southern peonage, urban sojourners—our problems have always been epic and we have always overcome. But first there must be vision. What exactly are the issues that we must address, what are the ideological instruments that must be forged to finesse the problems of our generation? What is the long game? What is the vision that guides us?

Once again, we are standing at a crossroads. Who shall show the way? It is in the works of struggle that the answers will be found. It is in the works of struggle that we will find the visions that shape our destiny. *A luta continua.*

Arthur Flowers is the author of De Mojo Blues *and* Another Good-Loving Blues. *He teaches creative writing at Syracuse University.*

David Walker's Appeal in Four Articles, Together with a Preamble, to the Coloured Citizens of the World (1829)

David Walker

Essay

S elf-published in 1829 and distributed to slaves throughout
southern plantations through ingenious methods, Walker's
Appeal caused a firestorm reaction among southern slaveholders.
The subversive intent of *Appeal,* which called for violent resistance against slavery, made Walker a marked man. His appeal to
resistance was not rooted solely in retribution. Walker based his
arguments on biblical and historical examples of resistance. He
was truly committed to social change but keenly aware of the
radical means required to achieve it. Walker's *Appeal* can be said
to be an early African American precursor to Malcolm's *By Any
Means Necessary* or *The Ballot or the Bullet*—a fearless cry for freedom, by any means necessary.

But while *Appeal*'s fame rests on its militancy, Walker was not
a simple bomb-throwing revolutionary. Like Frederick Douglass,
Martin Luther King, and innumerable other African American
activists who would follow, Walker firmly believed in and based
his arguments on the same principles that white Americans so
righteously claimed: those found in the Bible and in the U.S.
Constitution. But Walker was a realist; he held out faint hope that
white Americans would, on their own, ever hold to the principles
of their sacred and civic scriptures. Walker also showed his
thoughtfulness by providing in his *Appeal* a program for the
development of his people after the abolition of slavery.

Unfortunately, what "appealed" most to the authorities of
the time was Walker's death. A price was put on his head and he

was found dead in June of 1830, an apparent victim of poison. Still, upon reading Walker's *Appeal,* the white aristocracy was put on notice—the days of the slaver were numbered. Less than a year and a half after the publication of Walker's work, Nat Turner's rebellion demonstrated in action the commitment to liberation that Walker articulated with such fire in his *Appeal.*

Are we MEN!!—I ask you, O my brethren! are we MEN? . . . The whites have always been an unjust, jealous, unmerciful, avaricious and blood-thirsty set of beings, always seeking after power and authority.—We view them all over the confederacy of Greece, where they were first known to be anything, (in consequence of education) we see them there, cutting each other's throats— trying to subject each other to wretchedness and misery—to effect which, they used all kinds of deceitful, unfair, and unmerciful means. . . . Now suppose God were to give them more sense, what would they do? If it were possible, would they not *dethrone* Jehovah and seat themselves upon his throne?

—from *David Walker's Appeal*

The Philosophy and Opinions of Marcus Garvey; or Africa for the Africans (1923)

Marcus Garvey
Nonfiction

Marcus Mosiah Garvey, a Jamaican by birth, was the founder of international back-to-Africa movements for the racial emancipation of blacks—the United Negro Improvement Association (UNIA) and African Communities League (ACL).

After World War I, Garvey emerged as the militant voice of "Africa for the Africans." His message of racial unity (and segregation) was welcomed by blacks and confirmed by other nationalist movements of the day. On this tidal wave of support, Garvey was able to raise several million dollars and establish Harlem's thirty or so square blocks, where UNIA was headquartered, as the capital of the black world. But as quickly as Garvey rose, he was toppled. He went from obscurity to messiah to convicted felon within five years. He was arrested by federal authorities in 1922 and charged with misusing funds intended to establish Black Star, an African American steamship company whose intended purpose was the repatriation of African Americans to Africa. He was sent to a federal penitentiary in February 1925. After serving two years of his five-year sentence, he was deported back to Jamaica, never to return.

These speeches and articles are Garvey's thoughts on everything from education to miscegenation, to prejudice, radicalism, government, power, poverty, slavery, propaganda, war, and ideals. Amy Jacques-Garvey, Garvey's second wife, published *Philosophy and Opinions* "to keep a personal record of the opinions and sayings of my husband. . . . In order to give to the public an opportunity of studying and forming an opinion of him; not from inflated and misleading newspaper and magazine articles, but from expressions of thoughts enunciated by him in defense of his oppressed and struggling race; so that by his own words he may be judged. . . ."

Black Bourgeoisie (1957)

E. Franklin Frazier
Nonfiction

When it was first published in 1957, *Black Bourgeoisie* was simultaneously revered and reviled because it cast a critical eye on one of the cornerstones of the black American community—its middle class. In the 1950s, before the recent burgeoning of the black middle class, Frazier identified the problems that occur in the aftermath of "black-flight" from the inner cities and black communities of the rural South. The book's relevance has only increased as over the years the divide between increasingly prosperous middle-class blacks and their increasingly desperate "underclass" brethren has grown into an almost uncrossable chasm.

By tracing the evolution of the black bourgeoisie, from the segregated South to the integrated North, Frazier shows how the blacks who comprised the middle class have lost their cohesion by moving out of black communities and attempting to integrate white communities. The result of this integration "is an anomalous bourgeois class with no identity, built on self-sustaining myths of black business and society, silently undermined by a collective, debilitating inferiority complex." Frazier hoped to dispel the image of blacks as having thrown off the psychological and economical ravages of slavery to become economically powerful, because according to Frazier, it was a lie that was damaging the community.

Frazier, chairman of the Department of Sociology at Howard University and president of the International Society for the Scientific Study of Race Relations, hoped that *Black Bourgeoisie* would impel blacks to make changes that would empower their community. For the most part, those hoped-for changes have not occurred. Nevertheless, today, as many black people are calling into question the very existence and relevance of an autonomous "black community," his book offers a fascinating perspective on the costs of that community's dissolution.

Since Emancipation, Negroes had been outsiders in American society. Negroes were not only at the bottom of the economic ladder but all the pretended economic gains which Negroes were supposed to have made had not changed fundamentally their relative economic position in American life. The new Negro middle-class was comprised entirely of wage earners and salaried professionals and the so-called Negro business enterprises amounted to practically nothing in the American economy.

—from *Black Bourgeoisie*

The Fire Next Time (1963)

James Baldwin
Essays

"God gave Noah the rainbow sign, No more water, the fire next time!"

S o opens James Baldwin's *The Fire Next Time*. It comprises two previously published essays in the form of personal letters. The first is a letter to his nephew written on the hundredth anniversary of the Emancipation Proclamation that attacks the idea that blacks are inferior to whites. The second, a much longer letter addressed to all Americans, recounts Baldwin's coming-of-age in Harlem, appraises black nationalism, and discusses in detail the connection between racism and Christianity. Written in the heat of the civil rights era, the book reflects Baldwin's passion for justice and his iconoclastic ideas about the revolutionary power of love in the battle for America's survival.

Baldwin spares neither blacks, whites, Muslims, nor Christians from his hard analysis. He condemns the role Christianity has had in fostering white Americans' sense of superiority and disconnection from reality. Baldwin sees Christianity as an obstacle rather than a conduit to better relations between the races. The black church, too, is guilty for encouraging self-hatred and despair among its followers. In Baldwin's view, the Nation of Islam's literally black-and-white theology, wherein the god-sanctioned racism of whites is reversed, merely appropriates the self-destructive tendencies of white Christianity. His frustration with racism is that it is a needless impediment to the true purpose of life: to explore the possibilities of existence with courage, to search for enlightenment that can be passed on to posterity. Willingly containing ourselves in the rigid, artificial box of race serves only to prevent

109

The only thing white people have that black people need, or
should want, is power—and no one holds power forever.

—from *The Fire Next Time*

us from finding real meaning in our lives and increases the amount
of needless suffering in the world.

The Fire Next Time is probably Baldwin's finest and fiercest
book. As a child, Baldwin was a preacher in an evangelistic store-
front church in Harlem; in *The Fire Next Time,* he draws on the
language and imagery of the Old Testament prophets to paint an
almost apocalyptic picture of American race relations. With equal
fervor, he paints a courageous picture of his unique vision of an
ideal American society, one rid of racial barriers and premised on
love and respect. The book captured the attention of Americans
in the throes of the civil rights era, and was an immediate bestseller when it was published. It is now regarded as one of the
most brilliant and important books to come out of that era, and
Baldwin's fiery plea for love in the face of hatred retains its power
for readers today.

The Black Jacobins (1963)

C. L. R. James
History

Haiti's revolution has always been a point of pride for people of African descent around the world. It was in Haiti that slaveholding European colonizers were finally driven away at the hands of the island's black population. *The Black Jacobins* dramatically and powerfully recounts the events that led up to the bloody and history-altering Haitian revolution of 1791–1803.

The revolution began in the wake of the Bastille and ended in the French colony of Santo Domingo, one of the wealthiest colonies in the world due to its rich natural resources and its importing of cotton, indigo, and coffee. Forever tied with the revolution is Toussaint-Louverture, a barely literate slave who united the slaves and mulattos of Santo Domingo and led them against the ruling population of the colony, as well as French, Spanish, and English forces, to alter the fate of millions of people and shift the economic currents of three continents.

"In 1789 the French West Indian colony of Santo Domingo supplied two-thirds of the overseas trade of France and was the greatest individual market for the European slave-trade. . . . The whole structure rested on the labour of half-a-million slaves." In 1791, after decades of inhumane and savage treatment by their "masters," the slaves revolted—led by one man, Toussaint-Louverture. "One of the most remarkable men of a period rich in remarkable men. The history of the Santo Domingo revolution will therefore largely be a record of his achievements and his political personality. . . . Between 1789–1815, with the single exception of Bonaparte himself, no single figure appeared on the historical stage more greatly gifted than this Negro, a slave till he was 45 [sic]. Yet Toussaint did not make the revolution. It was the revolution that made Toussaint."

The Wretched of the Earth (1963)

Frantz Fanon
Nonfiction

F rantz Fanon's influence on the thinking of the proponents of black power has been enormous. One finds references to his ideas in the works of authors such as Maulana Karenga, James H. Cone, and James Forman. An explanation for this can be found in the timeliness of his seminal work, *The Wretched of the Earth*.

According to William L. Van Deburg,

> . . . the ideological underpinnings of the Black Power movement owed a great deal to the conceptualizations of Frantz Fanon, a black psychiatrist from Martinique who had joined a career as physician/scholar with that of a political militant in service of the Algerian revolution. Fanon, whose work, *The Wretched of the Earth* was published (just before his death) provided black American activists with a compelling analysis of the consciousness and situation of "colonized" peoples everywhere. Chief among his teachings was that violence in support of political and cultural liberation was a positive force, one that was both psychologically empowering and tactically sound. Forceful opposition to an oppressive regime was said to reaffirm the humanity of the oppressed, allowing them to "experience themselves as men."

Armed with this wisdom, mid-sixties activist intellectuals began to speak of African America as an internal colony at war with the forces of cultural degradation and assimilation. By adopting variants of Fanon's concepts, rank-and-file Black Power militants were able to identify with the colonized of the Third World even as they affirmed the notion that violent acts could lead to both mental catharsis and meaningful political change.

Africa Must Unite (1963)

Dr. Kwame Nkrumah
Essay

Dr. Nkrumah begins *Africa Must Unite* with the words
freedom, hedsole, sawaba, uhuru: the slogans of what he
calls "the greatest political phenomenon of the latter part of
the twentieth century—African nationalism." The book reflects
the optimism and energy of the 1950s and 1960s, when many
African nations were, at last, throwing off their European colonial
rulers, and black people throughout the world were engaged in
movements of liberation.

The former president of Ghana, Dr. Nkrumah wrote *Africa
Must Unite* right after the country had gained its independence,
and he based his arguments and direction on the new perspectives
that opened up for Ghana at that momentous time. "The survival
of free Africa, the extending independence of this continent, and
the development towards that bright future on which our hopes
and endeavours are pinned, depend upon political unity. In this
century there have already been two world wars fought on the
slogans of the preservation of democracy; on the right of peoples
to determine the form of government under which they want
to live."

"Africa unite" was the chant repeated throughout Africa in
the late 1960s and used to bind all black and brown peoples
together. "The great millions of Africa, and of Asia, have grown
impatient of being hewers of wood and drawers of water, and are
rebelling against the false belief that providence created some to
be the menials of others." Dr. Nkrumah believed that Africa must
unite because all of Africa, no matter the enslavers, are enslaved
for much the same reasons: forced labor and subjugation for the

enrichment of other peoples. It was Dr. Nkrumah's belief that the twentieth century, a century of emancipation and revolution, would finally eradicate colonial rule and imperialist exploitation. His broad, Pan-Africanist vision, while still not a reality, remains an inspiration.

The River Between (1965)

Ngugi Wa Thiongo
Novel

A s has been the case for many of his fellow African writers, Kenya-born Ngugi Wa Thiongo has been at various times imprisoned, persecuted, and exiled for his writing and political activism. *The River Between* was Ngugi's first written, but not his first published, novel (*Weep Not, Child* was published in 1964). It powerfully tells the story of the inevitable conflicts faced by African society as it attempts to reconcile its traditional beliefs with the imperatives of colonialism.

The novel is set in the 1930s and 1940s in rural Kenya and focuses on the conflict between Christian and traditional beliefs. The story is set among the Gikuyu people living on two adjoining ridges, Kameno and Makuyu, which are divided by a river. The people of Kameno follow a land-based religion; the people of Makuyu are led by the Christian convert Joshua. The young and charismatic Waiyaki is sent from Kameno to the mission school to learn the ways of the colonialists so as to resist their claims to the Kameno lands. The conflict centers around the initiation rites of the Gikuyu people. Muthoni, daughter of the cleric Joshua, defies her father's wishes and participates in the ritual. She dies when her wounds fail to heal, and the rift between the two factions becomes irreparable. Politically, the Kiama, a militant antigovernment, anti-Christian movement, continues to agitate successfully. When Waiyaki falls in love with Nyambura, Muthoni's sister and Joshua's daughter, the stage is set for a tragic confrontation.

The River Between is a powerful and gripping retelling of the passing of the African traditional life.

Black Power (1967)

Stokely Carmichael and Charles V. Hamilton
Nonfiction

I n the late 1960s, as the struggle for civil rights—both between blacks and the nation and within the civil rights organizations themselves—escalated, activist Stokely Carmichael uttered a rallying cry that would signal a significant shift in the philosophy and tactics of some black groups involved in the struggle. Carmichael was the newly elected chairman of the Student Non-Violent Coordinating Committee (SNCC) and just released from jail for activities surrounding James Meredith's march. In announcing the expulsion of all whites from the SNCC, Carmichael declared, "The only way we gonna stop them white men from whuppn' us is to take over. . . . We been saying freedom for six years and we ain't got nothin'. What we gonna start saying now is 'Black Power!'"

That was in 1966. A year later, Carmichael, together with political scientist Charles V. Hamilton, coauthored the book *Black Power*, which presented what at the time was thought to be the definitive statement of a new "racial philosophy" and attempted to formulate a new approach that would enable blacks to solve the problems associated with their oppression on their own, without relying on the generosity and guidance of whites. Black Power was not, at least in theory, designed as a threat to white people. It was, in a sense, merely the latest incarnation of Booker T. Washington's gospel of self-help. Black Power was designed to allow black people, through their own institutions and organizations, to achieve economic and political liberation. The phrase itself was a brilliant use of language: the two short, punchy words together formed a vision of a radically different future for black people, who more often than not found themselves disenfranchised and on the wrong end of policemen's swinging clubs.

The authors were also internationalist in their view: ". . . Black Power means that black people see themselves as part of a new force, sometimes called the 'Third World'; that we see our struggle as closely related to liberation struggles around the world. We must hook up with these struggles." In the book's eight essays, Carmichael and Hamilton critique the political significance of various existing institutions with a consistent eye to their relevance to black struggle.

Black Power was one of the clearest manifestations of the movement's change of direction in the late 1960s. The change was significant: the language of militant black liberation soon replaced, and even discredited for a time, the language of nonviolent protests. While the value of that transformation is still being debated, the influence, and power, of Carmichael's hard-charging polemic is still being felt.

This book is about why, where, and in what manner black people in America must get themselves together. It is about black people taking care of business—the business of and for black people. The stakes are really very simple: if we fail to do this, we face continued subjection to a white society that has no intention of giving up willingly or easily its position of priority and authority. If we succeed, we will exercise control over our lives, politically, economically, and physically. We will also contribute to the development of a viable larger society; in terms of ultimate social benefit, there is nothing unilateral about the movement to free black people.

—from *Black Power*

Soul on Ice (1968)

Eldridge Cleaver
Memoir

S *oul on Ice,* written in 1954 when Cleaver was eighteen and serving time in prison for marijuana charges and rape, is a searing, groundbreaking autobiography of a life lived on the edge and without remorse. His story became one of America's great literary and sociological discoveries. With it, Cleaver triumphed as a cultural critic, a social commentator, a sociologist, and a writer.

After a series of religious experiences in prison, Cleaver became a Muslim convert, then a Muslim preacher of extraordinary eloquence and conviction, and then a firm follower of Malcolm X. He described his transformation through reading: "Through reading I was amazed to discover how confused people were. I had thought that, out there beyond the horizon of my own ignorance, unanimity existed, that even though I myself didn't know what was happening in the universe, other people certainly did."

Much of Cleaver's commentary was on target because he'd walked the road and he knew the signs, and he was a man who, if nothing else, called things like he saw them. "It may be that I harm myself by speaking frankly and directly, but I do not care about that at all. . . . I know that by following the course which I have charted I will find my salvation. If I had followed the path laid down for me by the officials, I'd undoubtedly have long since been out of prison—but I'd be less than a man. I'd be weaker and less certain of where I want to go, what I want to do, and how to get there. . . ."

Soledad Brother: The Prison Letters of George Jackson (1970)

George Jackson
Epistolary

That prisons have long been a means of containing black male self-assertiveness and anger is a self-evident truth to a large number of African Americans. George Jackson's *Soledad Brother* gives testament to this, as well as to the reality of the enormous power, talent, and intelligence being restrained behind bars. A collection of Jackson's letters from prison, *Soledad Brother* is an outspoken condemnation of the racism of white America and a powerful appraisal of the prison system that failed to break his spirit but eventually took his life.

At eighteen, Jackson was given a one-year-to-life sentence for stealing $70 from a gas station. In prison Jackson became radicalized and, together with another prisoner, started a Marxist revolutionary cell. Through a series of events, Jackson would be charged with the murder of a white prison guard and would subsequently be killed while allegedly trying to escape—despite the fact that all charges against him had been dropped. At Jackson's death, he was thirty years old. Twelve of those thirty years had been spent in prison, seven and one-half of those years in solitary confinement.

Jackson's letters make palpable the intense feelings of anger and rebellion that filled black men in America's prisons in the 1960s. But even removed from the social and political firestorms of the 1960s, Jackson's story still resonates for its portrait of a man taking a stand even while locked down. Although he was a naïve petty thief when he was first arrested, Jackson, like men from Malcolm X to Nathan McCall, found redemption behind bars. *Soledad Brother* was published in 1970; Jackson was killed the following year.

If I leave here alive, I'll leave nothing behind. They'll never count me among the broken men, but I can't say that I'm normal either. I've been hungry too long, I've gotten angry too often. I've been lied to and insulted too many times. They've pushed me over the line from which there can be no retreat. I know that they will not be satisfied until they've pushed me out of this existence altogether. I've been the victim of so many racist attacks that I could never relax again . . . I can still smile now, after ten years of blocking knife thrusts, and the pick handles of faceless sadistic pigs, of anticipating and reacting for ten years, seven of them in solitary. I can still smile sometimes, but by the time this thing is over I may not be a nice person. And I just lit my seventy-seventh cigarette of this twenty-one hour day. I'm going to lay down for two or three hours, perhaps I'll sleep.

—from *Soledad Brother*

Seize the Time: The Story of the Black Panther Party (1970)

Bobby Seale
Nonfiction

The demand for black power in the late 1960s meant different things to different groups within the black community. For the mildest of its mouthers, the slogan was a call for black economic self-sufficiency and political power within the American system. For others, it meant complete racial separatism and cultural nationalism. For still others, it meant a complete anticapitalist revolution in the Marxist model, except that where Marx thought the revolutionary vanguard would emerge from the industrial working class, Marxist black revolutionaries saw the revolution emerging from the black ghetto underclass. The Black Panthers, who were believed by many to be the most aggressively militant and revolutionary of the black organizations of the period, embraced the latter position.

Seize the Time was written by Bobby Seale, then chairman of the Black Panther Party, to clear up misunderstandings on the part of the public by thoroughly explaining the organization's origin, activities, and goals. The Black Panther Party began in Oakland, California, in October 1966, founded by Seale and the late Huey P. Newton, who would go on to be its most visible and controversial leader. In contrast to the nonviolent methods being advocated by other activist groups of the time, the Panthers openly advocated the use of violence to achieve their goals, putting into action their interpretation of Malcolm X's "by any means necessary" philosophy. Starting from the theory that the police—the arm of the suppressive white establishment in the ghetto—must be monitored by blacks, they took to the streets with loaded cameras and guns, thus claiming for themselves and the black youths of the ghetto the respect and due process they felt was lacking. It also unleashed an era of increasingly violent activity by revolutionaries of all colors that was met with a fierce backlash on the part of the government.

Seize the Time was written while Seale was in San Francisco State Prison, during a period when nearly every black activist organization was under attack by government agencies. Seale's book is written in a language and style that reflect the urgency, passion, and justifiable paranoia of that turbulent era. While the Panthers were undermined by forces without and within, *Seize the Time*, with its urgent call for black self-defense and black pride, remains a compelling account of one manifestation of an oppressed people's continuing struggle for liberation.

The life and existence of the Black Panther Party, the ideology of the Party in motion, is a biography of oppressed America, black and white, that no news report, TV documentary, book, or magazine has yet expressed. To do so, the media would let the people know what's really going on, how things have happened, and how we're struggling for our freedom. So before the power structure, through its pigs, attempts to murder any more of us, or take more political prisoners in its age-old attempt to keep us "niggers" as they like to say, "in our place," I have put together the true story of the Black Panther Party.

—from *Seize the Time*

The Destruction of Black Civilization: Great Issues of a Race from 4500 B.C. to 2000 A.D. (1971)

Chancellor Williams
History

*T*he *Destruction of Black Civilization* took Chancellor Williams sixteen years of research and field study to compile. The book, which was to serve as a reinterpretation of the history of the African race, was intended to be "a general rebellion against the subtle message from even the most 'liberal' white authors (and their Negro disciples): 'You belong to a race of nobodies. You have no worthwhile history to point to with pride.'" The book was written at a time when many black students, educators, and scholars were starting to piece together the connection between the way their history was taught and the way they were perceived by others and by themselves. They began to question assumptions made about their history and took it upon themselves to create a new body of historical research.

The book is premised on the question: "If the Blacks were among the very first builders of civilization and their land the birthplace of civilization, what has happened to them that has left them since then, at the bottom of world society, *precisely what happened*? The Caucasian answer is simple and well-known: The Blacks have always been at the bottom." Williams instead contends that many elements—nature, imperialism, and stolen legacies—have aided in the destruction of the black civilization.

The Destruction of Black Civilization is revelatory and revolutionary because it offers a new approach to the research, teaching, and study of African history by shifting the main focus from the history of Arabs and Europeans in Africa to the Africans themselves, offering instead "a history of blacks *that is a history of blacks.* Because only from history can we learn what our strengths were and, especially, in what particular aspect we are weak and vulnerable. Our history can then become at once the foundation and guiding light for united efforts in serious[ly] planning what we should be about now." It was part of the evolution of the black revolution that took place in the 1970s, as the focus shifted from politics to matters of the mind.

The Spook Who Sat by the Door (1973)

Sam Greenlee
Novel

T *he Spook Who Sat by the Door* was originally brought into print by a small publisher, Richard Baron Press, and quickly became an underground favorite. Published in the near aftermath of the Black Power movement, *The Spook* fictionalized the urban-based war for liberation that never quite manifested.

Senator Gilbert Hennington is in a close race for reelection and needs an issue with which to galvanize the Negro vote. His answer: a public call for the integration of the heretofore lily-white Central Intelligence Agency (at its Field Operatives level). Of the hundreds who applied, twenty-three are chosen for training under express orders that no one successfully complete the course. With the exception of one, Dan Freeman, they are eliminated. Exasperated at Freeman's tenacity, Calhoun, the agency's judo instructor, tells him, "I'm going to give you a chance. You just walk up to the head office and resign and that will be it. Otherwise, we fight until you do. And you will not leave this room until I have whipped you and you walk out of here, or crawl out of here, or are carried out of here and resign. Do I make myself clear?" Midway through the fight, "Freeman wondered if he could keep from killing this white man. No, he thought, he's not worth it. . . . But he does have an ass-kicking coming and he can't handle it. This cat can't believe a nigger can whip him. Well, he'll believe it when I'm through. . . ."

Freeman is never assigned to the field, but is given a glass-enclosed office where he sits in display. But he has a plan and soon resigns, returning to Chicago to organize the Cobras, a street gang, into an armed and skilled insurgency unit. On a hot Chicago night, a police killing sparks the riot that becomes the war led by Freeman and the Cobras, now dubbed Uncle Tom and the Freedom Fighters. Fast-paced, well written, entertaining, memorable.

Notes of a Hanging Judge (1990)

Stanley Crouch

Essays

P *rovocative* is the word most frequently attached to the writings of Stanley Crouch, one of America's finest cultural critics. Crouch's essays are written with cool assurance and precision, but they always pack a punch for his favorite targets, from "racial hustlers" and cheap media products to knee-jerk identity politicians and historic revisionists. No matter what the topic—jazz, media, literature, film, history, politics—Crouch's biting, iconoclastic essays land with metronomic regularity on the same fundamental issue: the importance of black people taking their rightful and hard-earned place at the table of American culture and democracy, instead of insisting on a contrived outsider pose and wallowing in unnecessary martyrdom.

The essays in *Notes of a Hanging Judge* were written between 1979 and 1988—years when many of the gains of the civil rights era were being overturned by the Reagan administration and the so-called Culture Wars were just starting to heat up. Crouch's essays capture the intellectual ferment of the era, offering trenchant criticism on emerging cultural trends and milestone moments in film, literature, and politics. One of his most memorable essays, "Nationalism of Fools," is a biting profile of a 1985 Nation of Islam rally led by Minister Louis Farrakhan at Madison Square Garden. Typical of Crouch's approach, he mocks what he considers Farrakhan and the Nation's "muddled" ideology and senseless anti-Semitism, but also thoughtfully considers why such a message and messenger could attract 25,000 people at that historical juncture.

Other essays attach other black cultural totems of the 1980s: "Aunt Medea" argues that Toni Morrison's much-praised *Beloved*

127

"explains black behavior in terms of social conditioning, as if list-
ing atrocities solves the mystery of human motive and behavior."
In "Do the Race Thing," he derides Spike Lee's film *Do the Right
Thing* as "the convention of a new black exploitation film." And
in "Man in the Mirror," he takes the unusual stance of defending
Michael Jackson's extensive plastic surgery by placing it within
the context of the American and African American tradition of
improvisation: "The American dream is actually the idea that an
identity can be improvised and can function socially if it doesn't
intrude upon the freedom of anyone else."

It will be hard to find many people who agree with Crouch
on every point; his ideas can raise the hackles of conservatives and
liberals alike. And his essays can sometimes seem unnecessarily
curmudgeonly—sometimes almost mean-spirited. Nevertheless,
his often surprising essays, argued in lively and enjoyably rich
prose in this collection, are essential to anyone who values serious
ideas.

Race Matters (1993)

Cornel West
Nonfiction

C ornel West is one of the most recognized of American public intellectuals. His message of social liberation, rooted deeply in the black Baptist tradition, strikes a chord among an audience of lay readers and academics because it is equally intellectual and accessible. And because of its inherent humanism, it crosses racial and cultural lines as well.

In *Race Matters,* West asks for a renewed engagement on the question of race and presents a bracing call to action to establish a new framework from which to discuss the issue. West believes race represents a dire paradox for the nation: either America recognizes the comon humanity of all of its citizens, acknowledges its spiritual impoverishment, and overturns a political environment dominated by image rather than substance, or it risks the unmaking of the democratic order.

Ours is a crisis, contends West, that evolves in large measure from the predominantly market-driven American way of life. The attendant emphasis on individuality and competition renders traditional black communal life ineffective and leads to the denigration of black people. This situation, West explains, creates not just a social and political crisis in the black community, but a deep existential crisis as well:

> Under these circumstances black existential angst derives from the lived experience of ontological wounds and emotional scars inflicted by white supremacist beliefs and images permeating U.S. society and culture. These beliefs and images attack black intelligence, black ability, black beauty, and black character daily in subtle and not-so-subtle ways. . . . The accumulated effect of the black wounds and scars suffered in a white-dominated

society is a deep-seated anger, a boiling sense of rage, and a passionate pessimism regarding America's will to justice.

Thus, centuries into the African American experience, more than one hundred years after the abolition of slavery, and decades after the major battles of the civil rights movement, race, contends West, still matters.

God's Bits of Wood (1996)

Sembene Ousmane
Novel

S embene Ousmane, the author of several novels written in
France, is Senegalese by birth. *God's Bits of Wood* tells the
story of the bloody and tragic workers' strike on the Dakar-Niger
railway in 1947.

Ousmane captures the spirit of the West African people in
their conflict with the colonial powers. Their mistreatment at the
hands of their employer is cast in both race and class terms: "We
are being robbed. We do the same work the white men do. Why
then should they be paid more? In what way is a white worker
better than a black worker? Only the engines we run tell the
truth—and they don't know the difference between a white man
and a black. If we want to live decently we must fight!"

Ousmane's writing is crisp and textural, as you would expect
from an author who is also one of Africa's best-known film-
makers: "The last rays of the sun filtered through a shredded
lacework of clouds. To the west, waves of mist spun slowly away,
and at the very center of the vast mauve and indigo arch of sky
the great crimson orb grew steadily larger. The roofs, the thorny
minarets of the mosques, the trees—silk-cotton, flame, and
mahogany—the wall, the ochered ground; all caught fire."

God's Bits of Wood honestly portrays the ambivalence between
the Africans and the encroaching French and between the Africans themselves. "Among my people, no one speaks the white
man's language, and no one has died of it! Ever since I was born—
and God knows that was a long time ago—I have never heard of
a white man who had learned to speak Bambara, or any other
language of this country. But you rootless people think only of

learning his, while our language dies." Although this particular pitched battle between the forces of colonialism and the forces of revolution comes to a disappointing end, Ousmane's depiction of the spirit of the people makes it clear that the fight to reclaim their language, land, and labor is far from over.

Soul and Spirit

Commentary

by Hazel Reid

I have a dream today . . . I have a dream that one day all
God's children, black men and white men, Jews and Gentiles,
Protestants and Catholics, will be able to join hands and sing in
the words of the old Negro spiritual, "Free at last! Free at last!
Thank God Almighty, we are free at last!"
                                        —The Rev. Dr. Martin Luther King Jr.

The twentieth century has ended, leaving behind its monumental
symbols of achievements in material progress—its icons of industrial, scientific, and technological advancement. It is also leaving a
legacy of wars, a highly polluted earth and atmosphere, systems
of serious economic and social inequalities and related problems
that hinder the progress of human development, and an increasing human loss of a sense of connectedness with the spiritual
source of life. In this period of millennium transition, the question is: What will be the major achievements of this next era?
Responses to this question include predictions such as unimagin-
able progress in technology; the replacement of money with
electronic systems of economic exchange; major medical develop-
ments, especially the uncovering of the complete genetic makeup
of humans and other species; the production of more sophisticated weapons of war; and successful communication with extra-
terrestrial beings. However, the twenty-first century also holds
out the possibility of significant progress in the spiritual evolution
and liberation of the human species.

In the face of the troubled state of the world in which we live
and of predictions for deteriorating human relationships and even
the earth's destruction—this is a magnificent promise. It prompts
the further question: Who would be the most likely to want to
serve as agents of this spiritual approach to human liberation? It

135

would not likely be those who have profited most from the tangible material advancements of the last several centuries and place greatest value on material goods. The people who would be most likely to grasp at hope in a spiritual model for liberation would have to be those who have suffered the greatest exploitation during the past centuries of scientific and technological advancements. From this point of view, peoples in the Pan-African world should be among the most likely to see hope in this prophecy. For us, as for other oppressed peoples, the spiritual approach is not new. We have established a substantial track record in using spirit as a means to endure, survive, and achieve extraordinary accomplishments.

Scientists and other skeptics tend to approach the idea of spirit as superstition, since they cannot see it, cannot touch it, and cannot examine it under available microscopes. However, logic suggests that the universal attempt to use spirit to explain human problems and direct human destiny is far too significant to be dismissed as mere superstition and ignorance. Those attempts are often captured in our greatest literature on the spirit.

The track record we have established in using the spirit to solve human problems includes the following examples:

• *African spiritual tradition*   In Pan-African cultures, we have developed models of holy spaces where we can go for healing—both physical and spiritual. Such models have been developed by people who practice the traditional African religions, as well as modifications of them such as Santeria, voodoo, and obeah.

• *Christian churches*   The African models of spirituality have been carried over to the black church as well, those holy grounds for healing and sustenance where the faithful congregate for prayers, singing, dancing, laying on of hands, and testifying. Churches have played a major role in the liberation of African peoples in the Western world from slavery to the present. James Cone's *A Black Theology of Liberation* and Samuel Dewitt Proctor's *The Substance of Things Hoped For* describe the varieties of ways that church can work to sustain and liberate.

• *Prayers and meditation* As a spiritual practice, meditation is most prevalent among Asian peoples, but it has also played a role in the lives of African people around the world. For many people, including the Hindus in India, meditation is a major means of uniting with the Divine Spirit, increasing spiritual consciousness, and seeking liberation from the human condition. Prayer has served the same function within the framework of African American religious practices. Two wonderful examples of how this has been done are James Melvin Washington's comprehensive *Conversations with God* and Marian Wright Edelman's *Guide My Feet*.

• *Affirmations* A phenomenal example of the use of affirmation is found in the works of Iyanla Vanzant, including her best-selling *Acts of Faith*. Her self-affirming and self-loving vision of the world is also found in her first book, *Tapping the Power Within*.

These examples are only a few of the many models that exist that can be examined with the goal to develop models of physical and spiritual healing of the world. Martin Luther King Jr. proclaimed that he had "seen the Promised Land," and even though he knew he "might not get there" with us, he died believing in its possibility. We certainly may not get there—at least not in physical form. But the least we can do is to think and act in creative and spiritual ways that will move humanity in quantum leaps toward a more just and more harmonious society. It is only in this way that we will be able to speed up the prophecy of Dr. King.

The books in this section that address the issue of the spirit as a means of liberation take different angles, all of which provide different perspectives that we can integrate in our search for freedom.

Hazel Reid is an educator and anthropologist. She is the author of Ritual for a New Liberation Covenant *and teaches English at the City University of New York.*

Jesus and the Disinherited (1949)

Howard Thurman
Nonfiction

Published in 1949, Howard Thurman's *Jesus and the Disin-herited* delivers a masterful interpretation of how God works in our lives. Thurman was one of the foremost preachers and theologians of the twentieth century, and much of his work centered on the relevance of the Christian message to the con-temporary struggles of black people. In this, Thurman's master-work, he argues that the Gospel of Jesus Christ is not just a map for getting to the next world, but a guidebook for the empower-ment of the poor and disenfranchised in this world. Thurman was one of the leading preachers of this new Social Gospel that even-tually flowered in the form of the church-centered civil rights movement.

Thurman identified the central spiritual problems faced by black folks as the overwhelming stresses of poverty, racism, and a sense of spiritual disconnectedness. He then turned to the life of Jesus as a primary example of the power of love to drive the spir-itual regeneration required to sustain a vision of God and self in modern society. The life of Jesus serves as a guidepost to the kind of love that is a hallmark of human spirit, success, and personal salvation. But Thurman doesn't believe that the Gospel only applies to the individual search for salvation: He also challenges our unconscious submission to the philosophies of individualism and insists that the Gospel is a manual of resistance for the poor and disenfranchised.

He interprets the life of Jesus within a context of the oppressed and offers incisive and liberating thoughts on man's most egre-gious of sins: fear, deception, and hate. Of fear, he says: "He who fears is literally delivered to destruction. . . . There are some things

139

that are worse than death. To deny one's own integrity of personality in the presence of the human challenge is one of those things."

While *Jesus and the Disinherited* was influential in shaping the philosophies of the early civil rights movement, it remains topical and deeply relevant even today.

Letter from a Birmingham Jail (1963)

Martin Luther King Jr.
Nonfiction

Martin Luther King's *Letter from a Birmingham Jail* was written while the civil rights leader was serving a sentence for spearheading the mass protest demonstrations of 1963 in Birmingham, Alabama. In it, King responds to a group of white Alabama religious leaders who had publicly urged him to limit his activities to local and federal courts. The religious leaders accused King and his Southern Christian Leadership Council of being "outside agitators" whose peaceful resistance could serve to incite further civil disturbance and rioting. King's letter from prison, which incisively laid out his brilliant counterargument, was one of the definitive writings of the civil rights era: It codified the methods of direct-action civil disobedience and offered a vigorous defense of its theological and moral foundations.

King's letter first laid to rest the idea that he was ever an "outside agitator"; how could anyone be an outsider to the cause of humanity? He framed the civil rights struggle as the vital struggle for human rights and godly justice on earth. He drew on biblical parallels and the writings of Christian thinkers, especially St. Thomas Aquinas, to make the point that not all laws enacted by humans are just by a divine standard. King was particularly harsh on these religious leaders for their desire to quiet him and others in order to preserve a facade of peace and civil tranquillity at the expense of true social justice. King could not imagine a Christianity that sanctioned, through inaction, oppression and prejudice against any of God's human creations.

Like the epistles of the Christian apostle Paul, the moral urgency of King's letter was only increased by the circumstances of its composition: In an author's note to the published edition

141

We know through painful experience that freedom is never voluntarily given by the oppressor; it must be demanded by the oppressed. Frankly, I have yet to engage in a direct-action campaign that was "well-timed" in the view of those who have not suffered duly from the disease of segregation. For years now I have heard the word "Wait!" It rings in the ear of every Negro with piercing familiarity. This "Wait" has almost always meant "Never." We must come to see, with one of our distinguished jurists, that "justice too long delayed is justice denied."

—from *Letter from a Birmingham Jail*

of his letter, King wrote: "This response to a published statement . . . was composed under somewhat constricting circumstances. Begun on the margins of the newspaper in which the statement appeared while I was in jail, the letter was continued on scraps of writing paper supplied by a friendly Negro trustee, and concluded on a pad my attorneys were eventually permitted to leave me."

The publication of *Letter from a Birmingham Jail* was pivotal in influencing public opinion in favor of the civil rights movement, and it caused the movement to receive both greater participation and greater financial support. Today, it is a reminder of the moral and religious imperatives that drove the 1960s civil rights movement and its brilliant leader.

A Black Theology of Liberation (1970)

James H. Cone
Essays

W hen *A Black Theology of Liberation* was first published in 1970, it was revolutionary because it claimed that white theology had no relevance as Christ's message because it was "not related to the liberation of the poor." It also asserted that "racism. . . . is found not only in American society and its churches but particularly in the discipline in theology, affecting its nature and purpose." Cone was among the leaders in the establishment of a black theology movement that reinterpreted Christianity as a tool for the liberation of the black community.

His message was the Christian response to the Black Power movement that emerged in the late 1970s. Like Martin Luther King in his *Letter from a Birmingham Jail,* Cone rejected any form of Christianity that defended the oppressive status quo, and he argued persuasively that the God of the Bible is first of all a God of the poor and of those seeking liberation from oppression. Cone felt that what was needed was a "fresh start" in theology that would arise out of the black struggle for justice and be in no way dependent upon the approval of white academics or religious leaders. "I knew that racism was a heresy, and I did not need to have white theologians tell me so. Indeed, the exploitation of persons of color was the central theological problem of our time. 'The problem of the twentieth century,' wrote W. E. B. Du Bois in 1906, 'is the problem of the color line.' Just as whites had not listened to Du Bois, I did not expect white theologians to take black theology seriously."

A Black Theology of Liberation laid the groundwork and sets the standard for that "fresh start." Cone's revolutionary work has been immensely influential among black ministers throughout the United States and the liberation theology movement around the world.

Theology is to put into ordered speech the meaning of God's activity in the world, so that the community of the oppressed will recognize that its inner thrust for liberation is not only *consistent with* the gospel but *is* the gospel of Jesus Christ.

—from *A Black Theology of Liberation*

Mumbo Jumbo (1972)

Ishmael Reed
Novel

I shmael Reed is a *different* kind of writer, and *Mumbo Jumbo,* a mystery, gives the reader a glimpse into his kaleidoscopic imagination. Papa La Bas, the founder and head of the Mumbo Jumbo Kathedral, is on a holy quest to find the sacred and ancient text of the Jes Grew movement. The Jes Grew believers are black, honor the life of the body and spirit, and praise through dance. Their philosophical nemesis, the Wallflowers, are firmly rooted in a Judeo-Christian belief system. Hinckle Von Vampton, a white man and member of the Wallflower Order, hopes to find the holy text as well, but to destroy it.

Central to the enjoyment of this intriguing and quirky novel is Reed's revision of religious history, slanted to a black point of view. The history of religion begins in Egypt with the black prince Osiris. His principal praise form was dance. His main adversary was his brother, Set (the original Evil). In form, Set manifests as conformity, rules, and censorship. Moses, a direct descendent of Set, surreptitiously acquires a written record of Osiris's ancient mysteries of nature, but does so during the wrong phase of the moon—that is, with malicious intent. He knows, then, only the opposite sides of the teaching. Reed postulates that the teachings of Moses, his Commandments, its "thou shalt not's," and the Bible are distortions of the text. Moses, and those who follow historically from him—Christ, the Apostles, and others—are impostors.

Reed's *Mumbo Jumbo* is irreverent, incisive, crisp, and trenchant.

Faith and the Good Thing (1974)

Charles Johnson

Novel

Faith Cross, a beautiful young black woman from the Georgia back country, was left little to live by. Her mother, Lavidia, left her with only this: Faith must find herself a "Good Thing." Faith does not know what this Good Thing is, but she knows it is what she needs to find the peace and happiness she so fervently desires. Before her mother dies, Faith is "saved," and at first, God appears to fulfill her need. But the satisfaction she derives from that episode pales in comparison to the expectations of the mysterious Good Thing. Dissatisfied with her first shot at salvation, Faith follows the advice of a seer, the Swamp Woman, and goes to Chicago to continue her search.

In Chicago, Faith falls prey to rape and gets heavily involved in prostitution, drugs, and alcohol. Her quest for the Good Thing leads her into doomed romances, childbirth, and a haunting relationship with a philosopher named Dr. Richard M. Barrett, who also searches in vain for the Good Thing. Faith's journey magically leads her back to the land of her youth and a realization of the Good Thing.

Charles Johnson, only the second African American author to win the National Book Award (in 1991 for *The Middle Passage*), is a philosopher at heart. In *The Good Thing,* Faith's journey represents our individual search for self. Unlike Richard Wright, concerned as he was with the external conditions that affect existence—physical salvation—Johnson, in *Faith and the Good Thing,* searches for salvation of the spirit. This seminal work, structured as a folktale, precedes by twenty-five years the queries and answers offered by "new age" African American self-help authors.

The Famished Road (1991)

Ben Okri
Novel

"To be born is to come to the world weighed down with strange gifts of the soul, with enigmas and an inextinguishable sense of exile."

Azaro, or Lazarus, is among a group of spirit-children reluctant to be born, tired of the constant cycle of birth and death, and the banality of the lives in between. Eventually, Azaro decides to once more allow himself to be born, reneging on his pact with his fellow spirits, but then lives his life straddling the physical and spiritual worlds, outwitting spirits who wish to reclaim him and dodging the pitfalls of his teeming Nigerian village compound on the eve of independence. Ben Okri's startlingly inventive writing is richly lyrical and filled with hallucinatory images of both the magical spirit world and the equally bizarre, and often grotesque, physical world.

Azaro is born into a village stricken with poverty, disease, and disaster and filled with political intrigue. *The Famished Road* is a series of tales that captures Azaro's enchanted world: the corrupt politicians, his besieged family, encircling malevolent and benevolent spirits, and the daily goings-on of his neighbor, all of which he recounts in florid language. This celebration, held at the local bar, is viewed through the eyes of the young Azaro: "The men danced tightly with the women. Everyone sweated profusely. The women twisted and thrust their hips at the men. . . . One of the women was practically cross-eyed with drunkenness. A man grabbed her around the waist and squeezed her buttocks. She wriggled excitedly. The man proceeded to grind his hips against hers as if he didn't want the slightest space between them. The woman's breasts were wet against her blouse." What follows is

147

a hilarious and masterful use of denouement, as pandemonium ensues, dampening both the evening and libidos.

About halfway through, readers may be startled, finding themselves no longer reading *The Famished Road* but listening to it . . . even watching it. And Azaro's father, the Black Tyger, is an event unto himself. Ben Okri, recipient of Great Britain's prestigious Booker Prize for his work in *The Famished Road,* creates an allegory of life whereby a river becomes a road that swallows its travelers, as life, voracious and unsated in its hunger, overwhelms and swallows those who travel its road. Life, proposes Okri, is a famished road.

Tapping the Power Within (1992)

Iyanla Vanzant
Nonfiction

*T*apping the Power Within was the first book by Yoruba priest-
ess and lawyer Iyanla Vanzant, author of the best-selling
self-empowerment books *Acts of Faith* and *The Value in the Valley*. *Tapping the Power Within* established Vanzant's deep spiritual
and emotional connection with black women everywhere.

The book, which summarizes Vanzant's twelve years of study
and training, is part autobiography, part self-help, and part diary.
Vanzant uses her life experiences to illustrate and explore the core
issues of a black woman's life: redefining the ideals of beauty,
friendship, self-love, empowerment, and forgiveness. With these
stories drawn from her life, she attempts to imbue readers with
knowledge of their own inherent strength and the faith to believe
in a higher power.

Vanzant's voice is personable and warm, and the power of
her work lies in the fact that she is the embodiment of someone
who has already tapped the power within. Her own troubled life
reads like a catalog of everything that can go wrong in the life of
a late-twentieth-century black woman: "At age 17, I had my first
child. At age 19, I entered an abusive marriage. At 22, I had my
first nervous breakdown. . . . At age 23, I began receiving public
assistance. At age 25, I was virtually homeless. At age 29, I was in
therapy. When I was 30, my husband broke my jaw, I had my second breakdown." Yet after all of that drama, she found the spiritual resources within herself to overcome it.

Her books broke new ground in some key areas and set the
tone for many inspirational and spiritual books—both fiction and
nonfiction—that followed in the 1990s. She was among the first

149

authors to reach a wide audience espousing African-based spirituality as a source of wisdom and guidance, as opposed to the traditional black church. She also directed readers to go inside themselves to heal their own torn psyches, instead of directing her readers toward outward political and community action. And Vanzant talked to black women about their experiences with familiarity, candor, and love that readers have responded to in the millions. Her vast readership understands that she teaches by example, that she has triumphed and has reached back to her sisters to offer the wisdom of her experiences.

Conversations with God: Two Centuries of Prayers by African Americans (1995)

James Melvin Washington, Ph.D.
Anthology

These 190 prayers, which span 235 years of African American faith in God, the church, and their fellowman, provide revelatory insights into the hearts and minds of African Americans. These pieces were culled from the work of historical and literary figures such as W. E. B. Du Bois, Countee Cullen, Martin Luther King Jr., James Baldwin, Sojourner Truth, and Alice Walker and from letters, journals, and newspapers from more obscure sources. Presented together, they form an undeniable documentation of the resolute and sustaining faith of African Americans.

Conversations with God is a glimpse into the divine because it illuminates the powers of spiritual perseverance while giving insight into the oratory and rhetoric of personal prayer. Washington explained the coherence religion brought to black life as follows: "The absurdities of racism insinuate themselves in conscious and unconscious ways in the lives of black people. Religion has been a central way for us to maintain our sanity." By presenting this collection of moving and powerful sermons, poems, and oratory, Dr. Washington also answers the perplexing question of faith: "Why do people who suffer continue to believe in a God who supposedly has the power to prevent and alleviate suffering?"

Dr. Washington, professor of church history at Union Theological Seminary and adjunct professor of religion at Columbia

University, has been an ordained Baptist minister for more than twenty-five years. Here he has given us an exhaustive and uplifting source of information and inspiration, complete with a glossary, a bibliography, and a contributors' page that is also an invaluable biographical resource.

Guide My Feet: Prayers and Meditation on Loving and Working for Children

(1995)

Marian Wright Edelman
Nonfiction

> *Guide my feet while I run this race. Guide my feet while I run this race. Guide my feet while I run this race, for I don't want to run this race in vain.*
>
> —Negro spiritual

With *Guide My Feet*, Marian Wright Edelman hoped to enrich the lives of children by educating the adults around them. "I set out to write a different book—a policy book—but out tumbled prayers instead." And who could blame her? Edelman has made it her life's work to advocate the enrichment of the lives of America's children, to ensure America's future. A longtime civil rights lawyer and founder and president of the Children's Defense Fund, she has taken as her mission the education of all Americans about the needs of children.

She states at the outset: "As I have grown older and wearier trying to help get our nation to put our children first and become more worried about my own children growing up in an America where morals and common sense and family and community values are disintegrating, I pray more and more." This small treasure of a book is intended as a spiritual reference of prayers, meditations, and personal faith in hopes that the rituals that precede and bolster these daily affirmations of people, family, and self will give black Americans and all Americans the strength to take active roles in their children's lives and, subsequently, in their own.

153

The quest to put children first has required climbing mountain after mountain, with no end in sight. It will require climbing many more mountains and endless work. . . . It will require personal and collective transformation and commitment by you and me to build a safe and loving world for every child—however long it takes.

—from *Guide My Feet*

My Soul Is a Witness: African American Women's Spirituality (1995)

Gloria Wade-Gayles, ed.
Anthology

M y Soul Is a Witness is a wonderful collection that speaks to the importance of religion and spirituality in the lives of African American women. Wade-Gayles frames the evolution of African American religion by showing the historical and contemporary ways that black women have expressed their spiritual beliefs. It is this powerful connection to the spiritual that has guided and protected black people, both individually and communally, through the most difficult of times.

Employing essays, poetry, and excerpts from works by various authors, the opening section, "Boarding the Old Ship of Zion: Witnessing for Our Mothers' Faith," sets the tone of this soul-satisfying anthology. Maya Angelou's "Our Grandmothers," Mari Evans's "The Elders," and Rita Dove's "Gospel" are poignant poems that help lay the foundation for our many manifestations of faith.

In "Testifying: The Spiritual Anchor in African American Culture," Wade-Gayles brings together, among others, the voices of Toni Morrison (an excerpt from *Beloved*), Carolyn M. Rodgers ("how I got ovah II/It Is Deep"), and an essay ("Sing Oh Barren One") from Bernice Reagon Johnson of Sweet Honey in the Rock. The unifying theme is the various ways that women have responded to a call from the Spirit.

Wade-Gayles explores every stone, every aspect of African American culture to show where and how spirit manifests. Margo V. Perkins's "The Church of Aretha" offers Aretha Franklin's ability to suffuse her melodies with the power of spirit as testimony to spirit in our everyday lives. The anthology also follows the

155

evolution of African American spiritual expression: "Challenging Traditions" speaks of a woman's self-discovery and empowerment; "Praying at Different Altars" reveals manifestations of Spirit in the Catholic, Islamic, and Yoruba religions. "The Healing Power of Affirmations and Rituals" introduces a newer, more modernistic approach to spirit. Iyanla Vanzant, Susan Taylor, Marita Golden, and bell hooks offer deeply insightful prescriptives.

The *Women's Review of Books* called *Witness* "a jewel which belongs in libraries, churches, classrooms and homes of women and men of all colors, cultures and religions." Let the church say . . . Amen.

The Substance of Things Hoped For: A Memoir of African American Faith

(1995)

Samuel DeWitt Proctor

Memoir

S amuel Proctor, pastor emeritus of the Abyssinian Baptist Church in Harlem, is one of the preeminent theologian orators and educators in the country. *The Substance of Things Hoped For* is the story of not only his personal and spiritual journey but that of many African Americans.

Proctor begins his tale with his grandparents Hattie and George Proctor, who were born into slavery, because he credits their hard work and determination with instilling the morals and values that enabled his family, although very poor, to flourish and succeed. "Faith put steel in their spines to endure physical bondage, and zeal in their souls to prevail against evil; it illumined their minds to keep the vision of a better day. . . . Faith gave them a sense of eternity, a mystical transcendence that transposed their pain into song and their agony into a durable, resilient quest for complete humanity, the substance of things hoped for." For his grandparents, "faith was a way out from the day to day drudgery and toil, an absolvement, a destination." His grandmother often told him: "No use fretting and crying. If you do your part, God will do the rest."

The Substance of Things Hoped For shows how faith has nurtured and guided many African Americans who hail from similar backgrounds. "The spiritual resilience derived from their faith allowed most enslaved African Americans to come through their degrading experience whole, without losing their humanity. . . . With nothing but faith they *imagined* the future. They fixed their trust in God and began their journey up the road to equality."

Sisters' Stories

Commentary
by Eisa Nefertari Ulen

Imagine the power of a woman born and raised in the midst of blackness, surrounded by blackness—breathing, living, spitting back—in blackness. Imagine that woman loving herself enough to love her own people. Imagine her strong, unattached, so free. Imagine her studying ways to study herself, to study us—using that knowledge to think and know herself, and us. She takes that back to the rich black earth, sucking the solos of people—a folk rich in blackness. Then imagine that woman writing. Mama Zora first gave us the glory of a life fully lived with her *Their Eyes Were Watching God*. That classic saw into the future of our very souls. It guides our feet by casting the footsteps Hurston's fictional Janie took as she strode into her life. Vital storytelling, talk that teaches, is just one signifier of the genre coursing its way through *Their Eyes Were Watching God*. Other signifiers strengthen the power of the tale. When the tale celebrates the cherished *i*, we learn the power of a selfhood that includes us all. Meaning is conveyed through color, context through aesthetics, and definition through beauty. Dusky spiritual power cloaks the soul in our stories, protecting sisters, enabling survival. And those women characters almost always connect to the natural world, as Janie discovers her emergent self in a budding pear tree. These are the signs that the writer is working from the particular perspective of black womanhood. These signs were first crafted with precision by Hurston, and her *Eyes* rightfully heads the list of essential Sisters' Stories.

It is this unmatched excellence that sent Alice Walker *Looking for Zora*. It is this same creative power that will strengthen your spirit as you read all the other women whose voices sound

161

for you. Acknowledge the power of the word and decode the messages these women have created for you. Tap the meaning and substance of voices resisting silence. If a book is a window to the world, then a black woman's book is a window to your self. Open it, read it, find for yourself, as Janie discovers, "There's two things people got to do for theyselves. They got to go to God, and they got to find out about livin' for theyselves." Live your life more fully because of the lessons learned in black women's fiction. The chants and spells, the whispers and sighs, the crafted precision, the bodacious war cry that *insists,* honey—tap into this essential power.

The spirit song generated by black women's writing in the United States, the Caribbean, and Africa has actually sounded for centuries. For the written word is rooted in spoken sonance, and women have been speaking in tongues since whenever. A collective unconsciousness crossing cultures and time feeds the muse that inspires the black woman writer. We can trace ourselves back to a Yemaya and know that virtue and sensuality are one. We can understand Ayizan and imagine the souk, the bazaar, the marketplace, the vegetable stand gracing a Sea Island road. Remembering that the continent gave birth to monotheistic faith, we believe in the magic that makes a virgin belly swell with life and push a son into the world. We feel the pain of a woman looking back, remembering the horror of a place where other women were ravaged mercilessly by fevered men, and, in looking back, turned to salt. We can believe one woman's body would be that deeply affected by her sisters' pain. No, we are not Lot. We wouldn't have left her on that mountainside, so close to the top. Because we know Isis could rescue her own child, seek out his scattered self, and bring him back together. Ah, yes, that's how we keep our New World families connected. We know the women of Zimbabwe; their name is Nzinga. We know the women of the Delta; their name is Hatshepsut. The golden calf of the wandering people, the sacred cow among the people of the caste; she is Hathor.

Islamic pilgrims still bathe in the waters the Creator sent to support a single mother.

It is in her richness of experience and heritage that lies the black woman writer's ability to transcend stereotype, to reconfigure archetype. This is her birthright. There lies her might. The essential sisters' voices are her fieldnotes, for she has traveled the world. And so shall you, reading the sacred word.

Too many of us are already young adults or even older when we first read about our very own selves. Too many of us remember our very first encounter with a book written by a black woman because, for too many, that moment took place in an age when clear memories form. For a little black girl to have always had these words around her, to have grown up in a place where black women writers were accessible, has been a weirdly twisted special privilege for far too long. "Sisters' Voices" spreads the word. If you've never known these names and titles, tap into the kitchen talk that has sustained you thus far. The black woman author has sat at the plastic tablecloth, too. If you've read these books before, read them again. Marvel at your new self as you bring recent experience to a page anxious to give you something fresh in return.

Sisters' voices soothe with the signs of a life worth loving. From sisters' voices glean the glory of a love worth living. Sisters' voices check the spirit and align the elements of selfhood. Feel a bound collection of black female imagination. Feel her weight. Now, listen closely. Fly through the lyrics of her song.

Eisa Nefertari Ulen is the author of the novel Spirit's Returning Eye *and a contributor to* Am I the Last Virgin: Ten African American Reflections on Sex and Love *and* Letters of Intent: Women Cross the Generations to Talk About Family, Work, Sex, Love, and the Future of Feminism. *She teaches English composition at Hunter College, City University of New York.*

Their Eyes Were Watching God (1937)

Zora Neale Hurston
Novel

I n *Their Eyes Were Watching God,* Zora Neale Hurston draws a sharp portrait of a proud, independent black woman looking for her own identity and resolving not to live lost in sorrow, bitterness, fear, or romantic dreams. Like most lives of black women of the early twentieth century (or any time for that matter), Janie Crawford's life, told here in her own sure voice, is not without its frustrations, terrors, and tragedies—in fact, it is full of them. But the power of her story comes from her life-affirming attitude: Through all the changes she goes through—once divorced, twice widowed (once by her own gun-wielding hand)—she kept a death-grip commitment to live on her own terms, relying only on her own guts, creativity, strength, and passion, and the power she drew from her community, to pull her through. In Janie, Hurston created a character that reflected her own strong belief that the most important mission we have is to discover ourselves.

Janie Crawford was raised in the household of her grandmother, Nanny Crawford, a maid and a former slave. Janie, like her mother before her, was born of rape, and Nanny is committed to protecting her from the sexual and racial violence she and her daughter endured. She pushes Janie into marriage with an older man named Logan Killicks, a farmer with some property. Her life with Killicks is full of boredom and hard labor, so she runs off with Joe Starks, a handsome and well-off storekeeper who moves her to the all-black town of Eatonville, Florida. Even with the prestige and security this new marriage brings, she is bored and unfulfilled by her stunted life with Starks. When Starks dies, Janie begins to live with Tea Cake Woods, a man who cannot provide

165

her with the stability that her Nanny taught her to value, but who finally gives her the passion and satisfaction she'd been looking for all along. Even when further tragedy greets her, she maintains a staunchly positive view of the future.

Hurston, an anthropologist and folklorist, fills this novel with shotgun rhythms and the poetic language of her native south. Language in this novel is crucial; it is through the beautiful self-made idiosyncrasies of southern speech and storytelling that Janie expresses her own will toward self-definition. *Their Eyes Were Watching God* has been called the first African American feminist novel because of its portrayal of a strong black woman rebelling against society's restrictions—and the received wisdom of her Nanny, no less—to seek out her own destiny. But ultimately, this is not a novel that looks out to the world to make political protest or social commentary; it concerns itself with describing the power that lies within us to define ourselves and our lives as we see fit, unbound and unfettered by society's limitations and prejudices. As Alice Walker once wrote, "There is enough self-love in that one book—love of community, culture, traditions—to restore a world."

"Come to yo' Grandma, honey. Set in her lap lak yo' used tuh. Yo' Nanny wouldn't harm a hair uh yo' head. She don't want nobody else to do it neither if she kin help it. Honey de white man is de ruler of everything as fur as I been able tuh find out. Maybe it's some place way off in de ocean where de black man is in power, but we don't know nothin' but what we see. So de' white man throw down de load and tell de nigger man tuh pick it up. He pick it up because he have to, but he don't tote it. He hand it to his womenfolks. De nigger woman is de mule uh de world so fur as Ah can see. Ah been prayin' fuh it tuh be different wid you. Lawd, Lawd, Lawd!"

—from *Their Eyes Were Watching God*

The Street (1946)

Ann Petry
Novel

A nn Petry's best-selling first novel, *The Street,* is the tragic story of Lutie Johnson, a young black woman, and her struggle to live decently and raise her son amidst the violence, poverty, desperation, and racial discord of Harlem in the late 1940s.

Lutie's marriage falls apart after she takes a job as a live-in nanny and maid in Connecticut, leaving her husband, Jim, and her son behind. When Lutie finds out that Jim "has taken up with another woman," she packs up her son and her things and moves out. She eventually ends up on 116th Street, signing the lease on the only apartment she can afford: three rooms in a building with narrow dark halls and prying, noisy neighbors.

Often compared to Richard Wright's *Native Son* for its stark despair, *The Street* was the first book by an African American female writer to sell over one million copies.

As for the street . . . she wasn't afraid of its influence, for she would fight against it. Streets like 116th Street or being colored . . . had turned Pop into a sly old man who drank too much; had killed Mom off when she was in her prime. In that very apartment house in which she was now living, the same combination of circumstances had evidently made the Mrs. Hedges who sat in the street-floor window turn to running a fairly well-kept whorehouse . . . and the superintendent of the building—well, the street had pushed him into basements away from light and air until he was being eaten up by some horrible obsession. None of those things would happen to her, Lutie decided, because she would fight back and never stop fighting back.

—from *The Street*

Annie Allen (1949)

Gwendolyn Brooks
Poetry

Ｎone other than the poet laureate of African America, Langston Hughes, declared Gwendolyn Brooks to be the most important literary treasure in America. He was not alone in his regard for this singularly vital American poet: In 1950, Brooks became the first African American to win the Pulitzer Prize for poetry, for her remarkable second book of poems, *Annie Allen*. Dominated by several long poems, *Annie Allen* is an epic cycle that describes from within the changes in a young woman as she moves from effervescent youthful dreams of romance, marriage, and happiness to the concrete reality of adulthood in the inner city's circle of black women. Like all of Brooks's poetry, it is steeped in the black world that she loved, but it addresses a theme with universal resonance: the struggle of growing into womanhood in a tough, uncompromising world.

The book is divided into three sections: "Notes from the Childhood and Girlhood," "The Anniad," and "The Womanhood." The sections trace the mythic journey of Annie from a child whose young worldview is heavily influenced by naïve romantic dreams to an adult woman whose sense of herself and the realities of her world have expanded and deepened. Annie, our epic hero, finds her dreams unfulfilled and her life constricted but strives to successfully complete the journey with dignity intact.

Brooks did not marry herself to any one school of poetry. Her writing style in *Annie Allen* was her own unique mix of traditional poetic forms and unconventional, intensely lyrical language that she drew from her black urban environment. And even though the poems in the cycle work as a cautionary tale about the dangers lurking in the path of young girls journeying

168

to womanhood in the inner city, she never compromises the complexities of Annie's life and emotions to make easy political points. *Annie Allen* is a masterpiece because of Brooks's commitment to authentically rendering the feelings of her heroine and the hazards and rewards of the world she navigated.

What shall I give my children? Who are poor,
Who are ajudged the leastwise of the land,
Who are my sweetest lepers, who demand
No velvet and no velvety velour;
But who have begged me for a brisk contour,
Crying that they are quasi, contraband
Because unfinished, graven by a hand
Less than angelic, admirable or sure.
My hand is stuffed with mode, design, device.
But I lack access to my proper stone.
And plentiful of plan shall not suffice
Nor grief nor love shall be enough alone
To ratify my little halves who bear
Across an autumn freezing everywhere.

—"Children of the Poor," from *Annie Allen*

Maud Martha (1953)

Gwendolyn Brooks
Novel

*M*aud Martha was the first novel by world-class poet Gwendolyn Brooks. It is the story of a woman with doubts about herself and her place in an indifferent world. It is also a story of triumph, the triumph of the lowly. Through Brooks's straightforward and honest portrayal of the novel's heroine, the reader is forced to come face-to-face with Maud Martha and recognize that her essence resides deep within every one of us. Within this honest and intimate story of one woman's struggles and failures, Brooks's incandescent poetic language shines through.

The book is not driven by any specific plot, but collects thirty-four vignettes from Martha's life, taking her from age seven to the time of her second pregnancy. Brooks focuses on Martha's domestic life, first as a child, then a wife, then a mother. Through the seemingly small but poetically described incidents of Martha's life, we see how her childhood dreams meet with disappointing results because she is crippled by her own poor self-worth and the incompatibility of her desires and her reach.

Critic David Littlejohn said of the book: "[Maud Martha] is a striking human experiment . . . a powerful, dagger of a book, as generous as it can possibly be. It teaches more . . . than a thousand pages of protest." Brooks herself has said that much of *Maud Martha* is autobiographical. She "didn't want to write about somebody who turned out to be a star 'cause most people don't turn out to be stars. And yet their lives are just as sweet and just as rich as any others and often they are richer and sweeter."

I Know Why the Caged Bird Sings (1970)

Maya Angelou
Memoir

"I am human, and nothing human is alien to me."

This statement as much as any other defines the uniquely expansive and knowing vision of Maya Angelou. In her works of poetry, drama, and memoir, she describes the imperfections and perversions of humanity—men, women, black, white—with an unrelenting and sometimes jarring candor. But that candor is leavened by an unusually strong desire to comprehend the worst acts of the people around her and find a way for hope and love to survive in spite of it all. *I Know Why the Caged Bird Sings* is the beautifully written and brutally honest chronicle of Angelou's life from her arrival in Stamp, Arkansas, at age three to the birth of her only child in San Francisco, at age sixteen. In between those two events, Angelou provides an unforgettable memoir of growing up black in the 1930s and 1940s in a tiny southern town in Arkansas.

Angelou vividly describes the everyday indignities pressed on blacks in her small town, whether by the condescending white women who shortened her name to Mary because her real name, Marguerite, took too long to say, or by the cruel white dentist who refused to treat her because ". . . my policy is I'd rather stick my hand in a dog's mouth than a nigger's." She also faced horror and brutality at the hands of her own people—she was raped by her mother's boyfriend when she was eight years old and later witnessed his murder at the hands of her uncles, a trauma that sent her into a shell of silence for years. Nevertheless, she emphasizes the positive things she learned from the "rainbows" in the black community of her youth that helped her survive and keep her hopes alive: Her grandmother, Momma, who owned a

"It was the best of times and the worst of times . . ." Her voice slid in and curved down through and over the words. She was nearly singing. I wanted to look at the pages. Were they the same that I had read? Or were there notes, music, lined on the pages, as in a hymn book? Her sounds began cascading gently. I knew from listening to a thousand preachers that she was nearing the end of her reading, and I hadn't really heard, heard to understand, a single word.

"How do you like that?"

It occurred to me that she expected a response. The sweet vanilla flavor was still on my tongue and her reading was a wonder to my ears. I had to speak.

I said, "Yes, ma'am." It was the least I could do, but it was the most also.

"There's one more thing. Take this book of poems and memorize one for me. Next time you pay me a visit, I want you to recite."

"I have tried often to search behind the sophistication of years for the enchantment I so easily found in those gifts. The essence escapes but its aura remains. To be allowed, no, invited, into the private lives of strangers, and to share their joys and fears, was a chance to exchange the Southern bitter wormwood for a cup of mead with Beowulf or a hot cup of tea and milk with Oliver Twist. When I said aloud, "It is a far, far better thing that I do, than I have ever done . . ." tears of love filled my eyes at my selflessness.

—from *I Know Why the Caged Bird Sings*

general store and remained a pillar despite the struggles of being a black woman in a segregated and racist southern town; the Holy Rollers of the revivalist black church, who used coded language to attack the racist system they lived under; and Mrs. Bertha Flowers, the aristocratic black woman who brought her back from her shell of silence by introducing her to a love of literature, language, and recitation.

Her mastery of language and storytelling allows Angelou to record the incidents that shaped and troubled her, while also giving insight into the larger social and political tensions of the 1930s. She explains both the worst aspects of her youth and the frequent moments of exhilaration with drama and vigor; it's in the carefully described details and minor incidents that her childhood world is brought to life. *I Know Why the Caged Bird Sings* was nominated for the National Book Award in 1970 and remains an immensely popular book among people worldwide to this day for its honest and hopeful portrait of a woman finding the strength to overcome any adversity, of a caged bird who found the means to fly. Angelou has written four follow-up autobiographical works: *Gather Together in My Name, Singin' Swingin' and Getting Merry Like Christmas, All God's Children Need Traveling Shoes,* and *Heart of a Woman.*

The Autobiography of Miss Jane Pittman
(1971)

Ernest Gaines
Novel

M iss Jane Pittman's American journey spanned over one hundred years, from the 1860s to the 1960s, and took her from picking cotton on a Louisiana plantation to taking part in dismantling the walls of segregation in her southern town. *The Autobiography of Miss Jane Pittman* is her story, told in her own words (although the narrator is putatively a high school teacher who comes to interview her for a school project but soon fades to the background). In Miss Jane, Ernest Gaines created one of the most memorable women in all of American literature. Although she witnessed firsthand the wrenching transition of a people from slavery to freedom, Gaines makes her more than a vehicle for that epic story. Miss Jane is a fully realized, three-dimensional character with her own loves and hates, strengths and weaknesses, which makes her observations on the incredible events around her all the more authentic and compelling. Gaines's skill in giving her a distinct and memorable voice with which to tell her story amplifies the humanity of Miss Jane.

When her story begins, Jane is a slave girl named Ticey, still working on a plantation in Louisiana as the Civil War winds down. She changes her name to Jane at the instigation of a Confederate soldier, a minor rebellion against her owners that costs her a severe beating. After emancipation, she leaves the plantation and joins up with a group of ex-slaves on their way to Ohio. The group is massacred by former Confederate soldiers, with only Jane and Ned, a young boy who Jane unofficially adopts, surviving. Jane then settles in Louisiana and serves as an influence for several black men who work hard to achieve dignity and economic and political equality: first Ned, who changes his name to Ned Douglass after his hero Frederick and becomes a campaigner for the most basic civil rights for blacks, but who is eventually lynched by whites; Joe Pittman, Jane's common-law husband and breaker of wild horses, who is killed by a black stallion; and Jimmy Aaron, a young civil rights worker born on a plantation in Louisiana, who becomes one of the movement's martyrs.

Miss Jane is a complex character, by turns superstitious and sensible, a survivor and a risk-taker. Through the story of her life, she speaks of tolerance and human understanding, commitment and sacrifice, human dignity and its price. With *The Autobiography of Miss Jane Pittman,* Gaines makes the small truths, the everyday pains, and the hard choices of this woman add up to moments of illumination. The book was a bestseller and was later made into a popular television movie, which won nine Emmy Awards.

for colored girls who have considered suicide/when the rainbow is enuf (1975)

Ntozake Shange
Choreopoem

*f*or colored girls who have considered suicide/when the rainbow is enuf is a dauntlessly provocative and forceful play about the difficulties of being black and female in the twentieth century. It is a "choreopoem," a form invented by its author, Ntozake Shange. It consists of a series of twenty poems spoken by seven women, each of whom is dressed in a different color: red, orange, yellow, green, purple, and blue—the six colors of the rainbow—and brown, a neutral color that represents the earth and flesh. The women speak the poems as monologues and occasionally as a chorus; they also sing and dance. Through their poems, the women share stories of the joy, pain, suffering, strength, and resilience of black women from an exclusively feminist perspective. Their poems use potent and often profane language to throw a spotlight on destructive relationships with black men and on the healing power that women find among one another.

The play opens with three poems about childhood and love, including "dark phases," a poem about the difficulties of growing up as a black girl outside the black urban centers of America. The second group of poems includes the lady-in-red's "latent rapist," a disturbing poem about the sexual betrayal of rape by a friend. The next group features the lady-in-brown's "toussaint" about her childhood fascination with Haitian revolutionary Toussaint-Louverture and her subsequent crush on a young boy named Toussaint Jones. Also in this group is a poem about three women who are seduced and then deceived by the same man, but who find solace in their friendship. The fourth group consists of four

"i had convinced myself colored girls had no right to sorrow /
& I lived // & loved that way & kept sorrow on the curb /
allegedly // for you / but I know I did it for myself // I cdnt
stand it // I cdnt stand bein sorry & colored at the same time
// it's so redundant in the modern world"

> —from *for colored girls who have considered suicide/when the
> rainbow is enuf*

poems entitled "no more love poems, #1–4," where the ladies
share with each other the pain and heartbreak of unrequited love.
The final group of poems includes the dramatic "a nite with beau
willie brown," about an abusive, drunken Vietnam vet who takes
his children from their mother and drops them to their deaths
from a fifth-floor window. The final poem in the piece is entitled
"laying on of the hands," a poem that affirms life despite the
losses, abuses, and rejection they've experienced: the poem ends
with the lady-in-red's memorable line: "i found god in myself &
I loved her fiercely."

Shange's work has been criticized for its stark, unsympathetic
portrayals of black men and its use of profanity, but it has moved
and electrified audiences from its first performances in a women's
bar in California to its award-winning run on Broadway precisely
because of its uncompromising point of view. Her combination of
strong language, imaginative staging, and decisively pro-woman
stance was revolutionary when this play first ran, and continues to
influence black women's drama and literature today.

Black Macho and the Myth of the Superwoman (1979)

Michele Wallace
Nonfiction

At just twenty-six, after working at *Newsweek* and teaching writing, Michele Wallace thrust herself into the literary and feminist spotlight with her first book, *Black Macho and the Myth of the Superwoman.*

In *Black Macho,* Ms. Wallace analyzes, from a feminist perspective, the sexual dynamic of the transition from civil rights to black liberation. "There is a profound distrust, even hatred, between black men and black women. It has been nursed along not only by racism on the part of whites but also by an almost deliberate ignorance on the part of blacks about the sexual politics of their experience in this country."

Wallace suggests that in the seventies the black man was feeling put off and put upon by the black woman's successes and began to believe in the myth of the black superwoman. He started to view her backbone, strength, responsibility to the family, success at finding and keeping work and generally getting ahead as her battling him "for his male prerogative as head of the household. And that she was as much to blame for the assault on black manhood as the white man."

Black Macho is bolstered by passages from the work of James Baldwin, Sojourner Truth, Norman Mailer, Daniel Moynihan, Eldridge Cleaver, Donald Bogle, Richard Wright, Susan Brownmiller, Tom Wolfe, and LeRoi Jones, as well as from historical documents on slavery. The book is so exhaustively researched and engaging that even if you don't fully agree with Wallace's argument, you will appreciate the passion with which she delivers it.

The Women of Brewster Place (1980)

Gloria Naylor
Novel

*T**he Women of Brewster Place* chronicles the communal strength of seven black women living in decrepit rented houses on a walled-off street in an urban neighborhood. Mattie Michael, the matriarch of the group, is a source of comfort and strength for the other women. Etta Mae Johnson is a free spirit who repeatedly gets involved with men who disappoint her. Kiswana Browne embraces racial pride and eventually accepts her mother's middle-class values. Lorraine and Theresa are lovers; when Lorraine is gang-raped, she is deeply troubled by the attack and murders Ben, who is one of her few supporters and the janitor of Brewster Place. Cora Lee loves her babies, while Ciel is on a path of self-destruction, having suffered a series of personal disasters.

The Women of Brewster Place is a moving portrait of the strengths, struggles, and hopes of black women. At the end of the novel, the women demolish the wall that separates them from the rest of the city. Gloria Naylor weaves together the truths and myths of the women's lives, creating characters who are free to determine the course of their lives, embodying the self-actualization tradition of the Harlem Renaissance.

Naylor's other books are *Bailey's Cafe, Linden Hills, Mama Day,* and *The Men of Brewster Place. The Women of Brewster Place,* her first novel, won the American Book Award for Best First Novel in 1983.

The Color Purple (1982)

Alice Walker

Novel

A lice Walker once told an interviewer, "The black woman is one of America's greatest heroes. . . . She has been oppressed beyond recognition." *The Color Purple* is the story of how one of those American heroes came to recognize *herself,* recovering her identity and rescuing her life in spite of the disfiguring effects of a particularly dreadful and personal sort of oppression. The novel focuses on Celie, a woman lashed by waves of deep trouble—abandonment, incest, physical and emotional abuse—and tracks her triumphant journey to self-discovery, womanhood, and independence. Celie's story is a pointed indictment of the men in her life—men who betrayed and abused her, worked her like a mule and suppressed her independence—but it is also a moving portrait of the psychic bonds that exist between women and the indestructible nature of the human spirit.

The story of Celie is told through letters: Celie's letters to God and her sister Nettie, who is in Africa, and Nettie's letters to Celie. Celie's letters are a poignant attempt to understand her own out-of-control life. Her difficulties begin when, at the age of fourteen, she is raped by her stepfather, who then apparently sells away the two children born of that rape. Her sister Nettie runs away to escape the abuse, but Celie is married off to Albert, an older man that she refers to simply as "Mr." for most of the novel. He subjects her to tough work on his farm and beats her at his whim. But Celie finds the path to redemption in two key female role models: Sophia, an independent woman who refuses to be taken advantage of by her husband or any man, and Shug, a sassy, independent singer whom Albert loves. It is Shug who first offers Celie love, friendship, and a radically new way of looking at

Well, us talk and talk bout God, but I'm still adrift. Trying to chase that old white man out of my head. I been so busy thinking bout him I never truly notice nothing God make. Not a blade of corn (how it do that?) not the color purple (where it come from?). Not the little wildflowers. Nothing.

Now that my eyes opening, I feels like a fool. Next to any little scrub of a bush in my yard, Mr. _____'s evil sort of shrink. But not altogether. Still, it is like Shug say, You have to git man off your eyeball, before you can see anything a'tall.

Man corrupt everything, say Shug. He on your box of grits, in your head, and all over the radio. He try to make you think he everywhere. Soon as you think he everywhere, you think he God. But he ain't. Whenever you trying to pray, and man plop himself on the other end of it, tell him to git lost, say Shug. Conjure up flowers, wind, water, a big rock.

But this hard work, let me tell you. He been there so long, he don't want to budge. He threaten lightning, floods, and earthquakes. Us fight. I hardly pray at all. Every time I conjure up a rock, I throw it.

Amen

—from *The Color Purple*

men, herself, and God. Finally, Celie leaves Albert to follow her own desires and discover her own talents and abilities. The novel ends in celebration: Celie is reunited with her sister and even the demonic Albert gets a shot at redemption.

The Color Purple is one of the most successful and controversial books ever written by a black woman. It was an international bestseller, won both the American Book Award and the Pulitzer Prize, and in 1985 was made into a much-discussed movie directed by Steven Spielberg. The movie and novel provoked controversy about Walker's portrayal of black men, which many found offensive and one-dimensional. Of course, Walker's book has out-lived both the movie and its critics; its no-holds-barred portrayal of black male-female relations broadened the trail blazed by her hero, Zora Neale Hurston. The novel is a wonderful fulfillment of its author's mission: to tell the untold stories of those black American heroes who withstood the gaudiest abuse a racist, sexist society could offer and emerged triumphant.

Praisesong for the Widow (1983)

Paule Marshall
Novel

P *raisesong for the Widow* is a novel full of music and dancing;
it describes the sickness that occurs when we disconnect
from our heritage and the healing power that comes from
reclaiming the music and rhythms of the ancestors. Its hero,
Avatar "Avey" Johnson, was a new character in black literature:
an affluent middle-aged black woman, a mother, a grandmother,
and a widow. Avey and her late husband worked hard to climb
from the slums of Harlem to the comforts of suburban White
Plains. But that material comfort brought with it a spiritual disease—a hard-to-diagnose but impossible-to-ignore malaise that
eventually erupted into violent illness during a Caribbean vacation. In this novel, Paule Marshall traces Avey's journey from
sickness to strength, from the soulless suburbs to the African
roots of her identity.

The novel opens with a curious scene: a woman throwing
clothes into a suitcase. Since her husband passed away, Avey had
been going on cruises with her friends from work, Thomasina
and Clarice. It is on a Carribean vacation that she finds herself in
distress and decides to abandon the cruise. She finds herself
dreaming of childhood summers spent in South Carolina with her
Aunt Cuney. Aunt Cuney used to take her to Ibo Landing to do
the Ring Shout, a ritual dance in honor of the Africans who were
brought to the Landing to be sold as slaves. Later she dreams of
her late husband who, in his drive for material success in a white
world, shut their lives off from the passion and sense of community they had once shared.

The next day she runs into Lebert Joseph, an old man who
listens to her concerns, diagnoses her problem, and prescribes a

cure: a trip to the island of Carricacou, where she undergoes a reunion with that part of her African heritage and traditions that she has allowed to lie dormant within her for so many years. On the island of Carricacou, Avey observes and eventually participates in rituals with the islanders. In one of their rituals, prayers and songs are followed by dances. Each nation is called on to dance, but Avey cannot join until they begin to dance the Carricacou Tramp, a dance she recognizes as the same Ring Shout she did as a child in South Carolina. With that, she is reunited with the roots of her own identity and that of her people. It is through the rituals on the island that she realizes the connective thread between the Ring Shout danced by church members, the neighborhood picnics and jazz music in Harlem, and the African origins of her people.

Praisesong for the Widow takes on a decidedly contemporary problem: the rootlessness of a generation of black women—and men—who forsook the traditions of the ancestors and the warmth of the community for a sterile and materialistic version of the American dream. In this novel, Marshall takes a character suffering from this modern dilemma and cures her by immersing her in a world of history, myth, and ritual. The novel is written so vividly and lyrically, one can almost see Avey dancing the Ring Shout and hear the drums in tribute to the islander's ancestors. The book won the American Book Award in 1984.

Sister Outsider: Essays and Speeches
(1984)

Audre Lorde
Essays

"The work of the poet within each one of us is to envision what has not yet been and to work with every fiber of who we are to make the reality pursuit of those visions irresistible."

Audre Lorde writes from the fabric of her life: black woman, lesbian, feminist, activist, daughter of immigrant parents, mother of a biracial child, cancer survivor. *Sister Outsider: Essays and Speeches* explores ways of increasing empowerment among minority women and the need for women to candidly deal with racism, sexism, and classism. It also promotes the unity of difference. Lorde explores the fear and hatred that exists between black men and women, lesbians and heterosexuals, and black women and white women and insists that we all must find common ground.

Lorde had an abiding belief in the unity of all peoples and the crucial role of communication in bridging the divisions that separate us. Rather than turning a blind eye to our different identities, she insisted that through the process of naming those differences and honestly and justly dealing with them, divergent perspectives could be brought together. Lorde's own identity crosses so many racial, sexual, and physical lines that in a sense she belongs to no one group and was thus able to see us all with a unique, unprejudiced clarity.

Sister Outsider covers almost a decade of Lorde's work. Nine of the pieces were written after she discovered that she had cancer. In the process of her coming to terms with her disease, she discovered universal lessons that we can all take with us in our struggles, whatever they be. Lorde finally lost her battle with cancer in 1992, but she has left behind a stirring legacy for us all.

Waiting to Exhale (1992)

Terry McMillan
Novel

T erry McMillan, in her way, has been among the most influential African American writers of the past twenty years.
Her novels are accessible, realistic, and often hilarious accounts of
the exotic rituals of modern, urban African American men and
women looking for love and happiness—a theme not commonly
found in African American fiction before her successful second
novel, *Disappearing Acts*.

In *Waiting to Exhale*, her blockbuster best-selling third novel,
four vibrant professional women console and support one
another in a nurturing friendship that helps each of them deal
with troubled relationships with men. *Waiting to Exhale* demonstrates that no matter how hard we search, sometimes Mr. Right
just doesn't show up, but that life goes on without him.

Even as the book was dismissed by some critics as popular
fluff or anti-male, millions of readers of all colors identified with
the struggles and the enduring sisterhood of Robin, Savannah,
Bernadine, and Gloria. *Waiting to Exhale* became a publishing
sensation, proving for once and for all that there is a substantial
audience of readers for popular, well-written African American
novels. The book also became a successful movie starring Whit-
ney Houston and inspired a flurry of knock-off books of lesser
quality.

Your Blues Ain't Like Mine (1992)

Bebe Moore Campbell
Novel

Set in the 1950s in Mississippi, *Your Blues Ain't Like Mine* begins with the murder of Armstrong Todd, a Chicago youth living with his grandmother until his mother can get on her feet financially. Mississippi is no place for Armstrong. Raised in the North under the illusion that blacks were free from racial intolerance, and showing off to a group of black men in a pool hall, he inadvertently speaks French to Lily Cox, a poor white woman whose husband, Floyd, owns the place. Egged on by Jake McKenzie, the black man who runs Floyd's pool hall, Floyd is forced by the code of the South to exact revenge. At the insistence of Floyd's father, Lester, and older brother, John Earl, Floyd has a fatal confrontation with Armstrong in his grandmother's backyard.

While this thoughtful and suspenseful novel appears based on the true story of Emmett Till, the fourteen-year-old boy brutally murdered in Mississippi in 1955 for allegedly whistling at a white woman, Campbell puts a keenly personal face—black and white—on the human toll of racism. Jake McKenzie, in his jealousy over Armstrong's northern mannerisms and in his own diminished sense of self, virtually assures Armstrong's death. Floyd is the reluctant captive of a racial code of conduct that demands an exact retribution. This is a deeply moving novel.

Kehinde (1994)

Buchi Emecheta
Novel

After almost twenty years living in London, Albert Okolos is forcing his wife, Kehinde, to return to their native land, Nigeria. Albert is tired of the democratic nature of London, "Stupid country, where you need your wife's money to make ends meet." He longs for the status and prosperity he will obtain in Nigeria and is determined to move his family back to the "home" neither he nor Kehinde remembers clearly and their two children know not at all. "After eighteen years, he pined for sunshine, freedom, easy friendship, warmth. He wanted to go home to show off his new life style, his material success."

Kehinde begins a journey of self-discovery when she leaves her successful career and her London home to follow Albert to Nigeria, where he has been for a year. She arrives to find that she has been relegated to a marginal position in his life, that he has taken a second wife who is already pregnant by him. Kehinde must pull herself and her life together and learn about independence and strength from the least likely of sources—herself.

Like Kehinde, Emecheta was born in Nigeria. At seventeen, she married, had a child, and moved with her husband to London. At twenty-two, she left him and finished a sociology degree while supporting her five children. Part fiction, part autobiography, *Kehinde* is a clever and insightful story about family, country, roles, and responsibility that clearly illustrates how things are rarely valued until they are lost.

The Daughters of Africa: An International Anthology of Words and Writings by Women of African Descent from the Ancient Egyptian to the Present (1994)

Margaret Busby, ed.
Anthology

Daughters of Africa is a monumental achievement because it is the most comprehensive international anthology of oral and written literature by women of African descent ever attempted.

The anthology is exhaustive in scope and expansive in voice because it encompasses authors from the Caribbean, North America, Latin America, Europe, and Asia and translations from African, French, German, Dutch, Russian, and Turkish languages. Each story, whether fiction, nonfiction, memoir, or poem, is a singular experience. Here, together, is the clear, concise voice of Gwendolyn Brooks; the forceful presence of Sojourner Truth; the rhythmicality of Nikki Giovanni; the sly, taunting voice of Toni Cade Bambara; the straight talk of Terry McMillan; the commanding presence of Angela Davis; the rhythmic dialect of Una Marson; the jazzy vernacular of Sonia Sanchez; the vision of Octavia E. Butler; and the careful, direct prose of Billie Holliday. Each story is enhanced by a succinctly informative history of the author's life and work.

The success of the collection is that it clearly illustrates why all women of African descent are connected by showing how closely related are the obstacles, the chasms of cultural indifference, and the disheartening racial and sexual dilemmas they faced. In so doing, the collection captures the range of their singular and combined accomplishments.

Daughters of Africa's accomplishment lies in its glorious portrayal of the richness and magnitude of the spiritual well from which we've all drawn inspiration and to where we've all gone for sustenance, and as such, it is a stunning literary masterpiece.

Sojourner Truth: A Life, a Symbol (1994)

Nell Irvin Painter

Biography

Sojourner Truth was one of the most notable and highly regarded African American women in the nineteenth century. Named Isabella, she was born a slave in 1797 in Ulster County, New York, the second youngest of twelve children of James and Elizabeth. By the time she was sixteen, she was almost six feet tall. Isabella changed names twice in her lifetime, not wishing to be known by the name of her previous slaveholders. In 1843 she became Sojourner Truth, a woman whose proclaimed mission was to "sojourn" the land and speak God's "truth."

In this recently published biography, *Sojourner Truth: A Life, a Symbol,* historian Nell Irvin Painter gives us incisive information about Sojourner's life; she also deals with fascinating issues relating to this woman's life—issues such as child abuse (that of Truth toward her daughters), sexual abuse (that of her slave mistress toward Truth), as well as the psychological consequences for women from these kinds of behaviors.

A woman of remarkable intelligence despite her illiteracy, Truth had great presence. Her voice was low, so low that listeners sometimes termed it masculine, and her singing voice was beautifully powerful. Whenever she spoke in public, she also sang. No one ever forgot the power and pathos of Sojourner Truth's singing, just as her wit and originality of phrasing were also of lasting remembrance. As an abolitionist and feminist, she put her body and her mind to a unique task, that of physically representing women who had been enslaved. At a time when most Americans thought of slaves as male and women as white, Truth embodied a fact that still bears repeating: Among the blacks are women; among the women, there are blacks.

With *Sojourner Truth,* Painter, a renowned writer and Edwards Professor of American History at Princeton University, has written a biography that is much like Truth herself: fiery, eloquent, illuminating, and succinct. Perhaps most compelling is Painter's demystification of the "Ar'nt I a Woman" speech that has come to be associated with Truth and with the image of her as an invincible black female.

Brothers' Lives

Commentary

by S. E. Anderson

True black manhood is not about projecting the myths of hyper-black masculinity or black hypermasculinity. It's about resisting white male supremacy's relentless attempts to humiliate our humanity and emasculate our manhood. Black manhood is not about accepting the myth that women are intellectually and physically inferior to men and therefore should stand and/or walk behind "their man." It's about recognizing our feminine equals, who have proven themselves as some of the fiercest freedom fighters, leaders, and thinkers over centuries of struggle for black liberation. Black manhood is not about smooth seductions and a perpetual readiness to "score" or "conquer" *any* woman. It's about recognizing mutual sensuality and respect.

Our existence as black people in the United States and in the modern world has always been at risk. The one thing that each one of the books profiled in this chapter shows us is that at the very foundation of black manhood is sacrifice. Sacrifice of the individual for the sake of saving the whole, for the sake of helping us all reach a higher understanding of a revolutionary morality—a morality that opposes the racist and sexist hypocrisy of a male-centered culture of rapacious plunder, narcissistic conquest, and bestial submission.

True black manhood is what you will find struggling to be in the books recommended here. This is by no means an exhaustive and definitive selection on black manhood, but the books do reflect—very powerfully—the realities, past and present, of growing up a black man in North America. Especially is that the case in the comprehensive and now classic *Brotherman* anthology. Some of these selections show us that if you take the American

Dream seriously, it can become an eternal nightmare in which you become the visibly invisible black male monster overflowing with sexual drive and criminal intent (see Richard Wright's *Native Son* or Wideman's *Brothers and Keepers*).

Other books, like *The Autobiography of Malcolm X* or Earnest J. Gaines's *A Lesson Before Dying,* show us how our ancestral strengths and intelligence help us overpower the racist drive to submit our manhood and maleness to the pale dictates of The System. Still others expose our deep loving side, our profound love for family no matter that the odds are against our survival. Valuable books not included here include Sister Louise Merriwether's *Fragments of the Ark,* which beautifully and powerfully depicts the maintenance and transformation of black manhood and family during the time of the searing Civil War. She captures the heroic dimensions of the brothers involved and also shows us the complex "sheroics" of enslaved black women determined to live in freedom with their families. Also, as an essential complementary reading, one should pick up *The Black Civil War Soldiers of Illinois* by Edward A. Miller Jr. This is just one source that documents the racist and degrading treatment of black Civil War troops as well as the oftentimes superhuman heroics of brothers fighting to free their brethren and sisteren—and themselves—from the white enemy: North or South.

True black manhood finds its roots in the horrendous experiences of the enslavement process. We can find insight and inspiration from works about slavery produced by our sisters; for example, the works of Toni Morrison (*Beloved* and *Song of Solomon*) and Margaret Walker (*Jubilee*). We are becoming more and more aware of the heroics of Cinque (Sengbe Pieh of the Mende People) and the *Amistad* 53. These proud young men and women were filled with fierce determination not to be slaves but to return home to Africa free. We are just relearning about brother John Malvin, a "free"-born African of early nineteenth-century Virginia, and his battle to remain free in pre–Civil War America.

Or what of another Virginian—brother Anthony Burns (*The Trials of Anthony Burns*)—born enslaved and escaped to "freedom," winding up in 1854 in Boston on trial as a fugitive from slavery? What kept them sane? What allowed them to laugh and joke? To have space in their souls for love and desire?

These were powerful men. Part of their power and determination to survive and fight for freedom came from that powerful African inner urge to be FREE and at one with nature. Their power also flowed from their acknowledging and respecting black women's power and determination to survive and fight for freedom. They understood not only the material basis of the African spirit-will, but also why our sisters were the guides and preservers of black futures.

We, too, can be powerful men today at the dawn of the Third Millennium . . . if we follow the simple yet profound dictates of these elders and ancestors: Respect and embrace our sisters as equal soldiers in the war for humanity.

S. E. Anderson is the editor of In Defense of Mumia *and author of* Black Holocaust for Beginners.

Native Son (1940)

Richard Wright
Novel

R ichard Wright was born in 1908, the first of two sons of a
sharecropper. After publishing his first novel, *Uncle Tom's
Children*, in 1938, Wright discovered to his alarm that "he had
written a book which even bankers' daughters could read and feel
good about." He swore that his next novel would be different.
That book was *Native Son*, the story of Bigger Thomas's short and
tragic life, which plumbs the blackest depths of human experience.

Native Son is told in three parts—Fear, Flight, and Fate—
which sum up, perfectly, Bigger Thomas's life. Badly in need of a
job to help support his family, the ne'er-do-well Bigger goes to
work as a driver for the Daltons, a rich white family. As he is
pulled every which way by his mother, "who wanted him to do
the things *she* wanted him to do"; by Mrs. Dalton, "who wanted
him to do the things she felt that *he* should have wanted to do";
by Mary Dalton, the young mistress of the house, "who chal-
lenged him to stand up for things he didn't understand"; and by
his need for independence and autonomy in the midst of a
dependent situation—he missteps, accidentally killing Mary.

Native Son is not an uplifting book with a happy Hollywood
resolution. It has been criticized for its cardboard portrayal of
black pathology and heavy-handed Marxist message. But the
book is an absolutely gripping potboiler that is also intellectually
provocative. It is on one level a seedy, simple story of an unsympathetic character meeting his fate at his own hands, and on
another an illuminating drama of an individual consciousness
that challenges traditional definitions of heroism, character, and
integrity. Bigger was less a character caught in a specific criminal
activity than he was a crime waiting to happen.

If He Hollers Let Him Go (1945)

Chester B. Himes
Novel

With his first novel, Chester B. Himes secured his place in the vanguard of the emerging young black writers of his time who were honestly detailing the rigors of black life in America. Unlike his contemporaries Richard Wright and Ralph Ellison, Himes was not a writer with overt political concerns. His novel does, however, delve into the existential cost that black men had to pay for the racism around them: that they had to live constantly, absurdly aware of the color of their skin.

Bob Jones's story is a simple one told in clear, direct prose. All Bob wants is "to be accepted as a man—without ambition, without distinction, either of race, creed, or color." But in the 1940s and 1950s, nothing was simple between blacks and whites. Bob quickly finds himself losing his hopes and ambitions as he is crushed beneath the weight of racism and discrimination. His life spins out of control until he hates everyone around him: the blacks for being powerless to change their lives; the whites for taking advantage of them. Bob Jones is every black man at that time, who was, every day, walking a tightrope of racial tension, except Bob falls, pushed by "a loose blonde who kissed him, then framed him on a rape charge."

If He Hollers Let Him Go is a masterpiece for its bitter and honest portrayal of the life of a normal black man in America, and it speaks to any person who has felt, at some time or other, that he or she has had enough abuse on account of the color of their skin. Himes demonstrated in the person of Bob Jones that one of the most critical rights that black people have been denied is the right to just live their lives unbothered and unmolested and to follow their impulses and desires with no greater reward or punishment than nature's laws of cause and effect.

The indignity of it, the gutting of my pride, what a nigger had to take just to keep on living in this goddamned world. The cold scared feeling started clamping down on me; it nailed me to my seat, weak and black and powerless.

—from *If He Hollers Let Him Go*

The Autobiography of Malcolm X (1965)

As told to Alex Haley

Memoir

*T*he *Autobiography of Malcolm X* is the story of one of the remarkable lives of the twentieth century. Malcolm X, as presented in this as-told-to autobiography, is a figure of almost mythic proportions; a man who sunk to the greatest depths of depravity and rose to become a man whose life's mission was to lead his people to freedom and strength. It provides a searing depiction of the deeply rooted issues of race and class in America and remains relevant and inspiring today. Malcolm X's story would inspire Alex Haley to write *Roots,* a novel that would, in turn, define the saga of a people.

Malcolm Little was born in Nebraska in 1925, the seventh child of Reverend Earl Little, a Baptist minister, and Louise Little, a mulatto born in Grenada to a black mother and a white father. Malcolm X quickly grew to hate the society he'd grown up in. After his father was killed, his mother was unfairly denied insurance coverage and his family fell apart. Young Malcolm went from a foster home to a reformatory, to shining shoes in the speakeasies and dance halls of Boston. After getting work as a Pullman porter, he went to New York and fell in love with Harlem. His stint as a drug dealer and petty crook landed him in jail, where he became a devout student of the Nation of Islam and Elijah Muhammad. That was when he figured out that "he could beat the white man better with his mind than he ever could with a club." Malcolm X's subsequent quest for knowledge and equality for blacks led to his unreserved commitment to the liberation of blacks in American society.

What makes this book extraordinary is the honesty with which Malcolm presents his life: Even as he regrets the mistakes he made as a young man, he brings his zoot-suited, swing-dancing, conk-haired Harlem youth to vivid life; even though he later turns away from the Nation of Islam, the strong faith he at one time had in that sect's beliefs, a faith that redeemed him from prison and a life of crime, comes through. What made the man so extraordinary was his courageous insistence on finding the true path to his personal salvation and to the salvation of the people he loved, even when to stay on that path meant danger, alienation, and death.

Manchild in the Promised Land (1965)

Claude Brown

Memoir

*M*anchild in the Promised Land is the story of the first generation of blacks who had left the South in search of a northern "promised land" of equality, abundance, and prosperity but found instead a vastly overcrowded and violent urban ghetto—a generation that went "from the fire into the frying pan."

"There was a tremendous difference in the way life was lived up North. There were too many people full of hate and bitterness crowded into a dirty, stinky, uncared-for, closet-sized section of a great city. The children of these disillusioned colored pioneers inherited the total lot of their parents—the disappointments, the anger. To add to their misery, they had little hope of deliverance. For where does one run to when he's already in the promised land?" So begins Claude Brown's literary masterwork.

Claude (Sonny boy) Brown wrote his extraordinary autobiography in his late twenties. At nine, he was a member of two notorious gangs who thrived on bullying and stealing. At eleven, he was sent to a school for "emotionally disturbed and deprived boys," where he stayed for two years; at fourteen, he was sent to a reformatory for the first of three times. In his mid-twenties, he would graduate from Howard University, and at thirty, he would start law school. *Manchild in the Promised Land* is the story of his life growing up in Harlem, to him a wondrous place where if you were quick, smart, and tough enough you could live, for a while, like a king or die like a pauper.

Brothers and Keepers (1985)

John Edgar Wideman
Nonfiction

S ometimes you *can* go back home. Of *Brothers and Keepers* John Edgar Wideman has said, "If I had a dime for every person who has come up to me and said 'I have a brother, or a sister, or a cousin in the same situation as you and your brother,' I would never have to write for a living again."

A collection of autobiographical essays, *Brothers and Keepers* is a story of a modern-day prodigal son. It is a story found all too often within a community in transition: two brothers sharing similar backgrounds, one remaining in the 'hood, the other leaving to travel the wider world. In doing so, however, the latter not only escapes the harmful influences of an economically impoverished environment but also alienates himself from the family, friends, and culture that fostered him. John Edgar Wideman holds the distinction of being only the second African American, after Alain Locke, the Father of the Harlem Renaissance, to receive a Rhodes Scholarship. However, it was the incarceration of Wideman's brother, Robby, that prompted him to relink his past by reconnecting with his imprisoned brother.

In *Brothers and Keepers,* Wideman tells of life in Homewood, Pennsylvania; of his conversations with his incarcerated brother; of his explorations of his guilt at having escaped; of his acceptance of the humanity of those he left behind; and finally, in his return, of the acceptance of his own humanity.

More so than any other writer, Wideman's public angst over his feelings of alienation with the black community, as well as his ability to resurrect the ties that nurtured him, brings the promise of hope and salvation to an African American community in turmoil. The price of the ticket may well be high, but you *can* go home.

Fences (1985)

August Wilson
Play

"There are only fences."

Troy Maxson is an angry man. He is an embittered ex-con who has built inner fences around his emotions that no one—neither his son Cory, his wife, Rosa Lee, nor his best friend, Jim—can cross. A proud and bitter man who was prevented by racism from playing major league baseball, Maxson is at fifty-three years of age a garbage collector. While his job allows him to successfully provide for his family, handling garbage represents for him a grim metaphor of his life. As he did during a bit in prison, he once again feels confined, and those who love him most, who depend on him most, suffer most for it.

Through Troy Maxson, playwright August Wilson personifies the man who grew up during the heat of Jim Crow: first proud, hopeful, and passionate in expectation; then emotionally withdrawn and disillusioned from incessant battles with life. Wilson also masterfully illuminates both the strength that lies within community and the adverse impact of a psychology of inequality that devastates the African American male and, in turn, his family and relationships, potentially disintegrating that same community.

Wilson's Pulitzer Prize–winning play offers a bleak picture of what happens to black males when their aspirations go beyond the fences within which they are confined. The fences of a racist society are compounded by the fences black men have often created to ward off loved ones who remind them of their failures. These fences only harbor pain and hasten an inevitable asphyxiation. *Fences* is a gripping portrait of a black man dying.

The Man Who Cried I Am (1985)

John Alfred Williams
Novel

M ax Reddick, who is a talented "black writer" in America but a literary *genius* in Europe, is trying to come to terms with his dilemma. Max is tired of having to accept that being black will always be the primary definition of his life—despite his marriage to a white woman, despite his literary talent and aspirations, despite his intellectual and social relations, and despite his "escape" to the European cities of Paris and Amsterdam. At the end of his life, cut short by cancer, Max decides to question all the things that brought him to where he is today.

Reddick faced the familiar problem of spiritual homelessness that has often plagued black artists and intellectuals. "I'm the way I am, the kind of writer I am because I am a black man. I've been in rebellion, and a writer, ever since I discovered that even colored folks wanted to keep me away from books so I could never learn just how bad it all was. Maybe, too, to keep me from laughing at them. For taking it. My folks had a deathly fear of books."

Novelist, poet, and journalist John Alfred Williams has created in Max Reddick an unforgettable character: irascible, fiercely intelligent, irredeemable, and honorable. *The Man Who Cried I Am* is a stunning chronicle of not only Williams's life but the lives of all black people who have refused to be victims: blacks who have had to leave their country to claim their individuality, intellectual independence, and rightful recognition, and who have always yearned to be "home" but struggled to find such a place.

The Life of Langston Hughes (1986: Volume I, 1902–1941, I, Too, Sing America; 1988: Volume II, 1941–1967, I Dream a World)

Arnold Rampersad
Biography

This two-volume set is the definitive biography of Langston Hughes, the poet laureate of the Harlem Renaissance. Beginning with a family history linked to abolitionists, the Underground Railroad, John Brown's attack on Harper's Ferry, and the anti-slavery settlement of Lawrence, Kansas, author Rampersad delves deeply into the context of Hughes's life. From his tumultuous relationship with his father to his travels to the South and abroad, to the largesse and patronage he received from admirers of his work, to his life as a Harlem literary cognoscenti.

That Hughes spoke eloquently for the black masses is well known. Less known are the interesting turns and connections that brought him to recognition. In *The Life of Langston Hughes,* the stories abound. While on a tour of the South, and as the riveting Scottsboro case exploded onto the international scene, Hughes visited the University of North Carolina at Chapel Hill. "Although UNC was probably the most progressive white university in the South, for a black speaker to be featured there was extraordinary." In advance of his visit, he forwarded an essay about Scottsboro: "Let the Alabama mill-owners pay white women decent wages so they won't need to be prostitutes, he urged. And let the sensible citizens of Alabama (if there are any) supply schools for the black populace of their state, (and for the half-black, too—the mulatto children of the Southern gentlemen. [I reckon they're gentlemen]) so the Negroes won't be so dumb again. As for the jailed men—if blacks didn't howl in protest (and

I don't mean a polite howl, either) then let Dixie justice (blind syphilitic as it may be) take its course." Langston "slipped in and out of Chapel Hill" before the response to the essay erupted.

This is a great biography of a complex man who lived fully in defiance of stereotypes of brutish and illiterate black manhood. His life was one of courage, adventure, and amazing creativity. Rampersad captures that life with memorable success.

Miles: The Autobiography (1990)

Miles Davis (with Quincy Troupe)
Autobiography

U niversally acclaimed as a musical genius, Miles Davis was one of the most influential musicians in the world. He was also famous for not talking, or for talking only in barely audible, cryptic, and ill-tempered riddles. But his silence only added to the mystique created by his genius with a trumpet. Miles was an embodiment of the arrogant, hedonistic, and immensely talented jazzman; he was also one of the icons of twentieth-century black life. His autobiography, written in energetic prose, is a brilliant telling of a one-of-a-kind life lived furiously.

Miles was born in Illinois in 1926 but grew up in St. Louis, where his father had a dental practice and where he first learned to play trumpet in high school. Miles Dewey Davis III was named after his father, who was named after his father. Miles's parents (his mother was an organ teacher) were married in Arkansas. "My mother was a beautiful woman. She had a whole lot of style, with an East Indian, Carmen McRae look, and dark, nut-brown, smooth skin. High cheekbones and Indian-like hair . . . I got my looks from my mother and also my love of clothes and sense of style . . . I got whatever artistic talent I have from her also."

Miles eventually became one of the premier jazz musicians of all time. The subject of several biographies, Miles here speaks frankly about himself and his extraordinary life: his drug problem, the places he's been, the people in his life, as well as the racism he encountered as a black man and as a musician. Never one to bite his tongue, he fills the autobiography with candid statements on everything from race to musicianship (and when he talks about the two together, as when he states that white men cannot play the guitar, look out). Quincy Troupe, a poet, journalist, and teacher who won the 1980 American Book Award for poetry, perfectly captures Miles's voice, imbuing the book with a crisp, clear, and melodious narrative. Davis may not come across as the most pleasant man on earth, but with his riveting anecdotes of jazz life in the 1950s and 1960s and his outspoken opinions, he is an undeniably fascinating character.

A Lesson Before Dying (1991)

Ernest Gaines
Novel

A Lesson Before Dying is a coming-of-age story set in a small Louisiana town in the late 1940s. Jefferson, a young black man involved in a shoot-out during a robbery, is convicted of murder and sentenced to the electric chair. Says the defending attorney to the jury, "What justice would there be to take this life? Justice, gentlemen? Why, I would just as soon put a hog in the electric chair as this."

Grant Wiggins, the hope of the community, has returned to teach school after having left for a university education. He fights internal demons, his aunt, and his guilt-ridden sense of community in deciding whether to escape the small town (and the small-town mentality) or to stay. He receives a visit from his aunt, Jefferson's godmother. With the pain of history on her face, the godmother spoke. "Called him a hog . . . I don't want them to kill no hog," she said. "I want a man to go to that chair, on his own two feet."

Grant's mandate was to instill in Jefferson a firm sense of self in the short time prior to his execution—a Herculean task, in that Grant had yet to come to terms with his own expectations of himself. In the end, and through their interaction, the two men come to realizations that allow each of them to successfully meet their demons.

In *A Lesson Before Dying*, Ernest Gaines personifies the angst of expectation that comes with being the first of a generation to succeed, the resolute power of community, and the importance of reciprocity—giving back to that which nurtured us.

W. E. B. Du Bois: Biography of a Race
(1994)

David Levering Lewis
Biography

I t took renowned biographer David Levering Lewis eight years to research and write William Edward Burghardt Du Bois's monumental biography. And it stands as a testament to the hypnotic voice and compelling vision of the man who was known as the foremost constructor of the civil rights movement.

W. E. B. Du Bois, born in Massachusetts in 1868, was imbued with a mix of Dutch, black, and French blood. Although he was born three years after slavery was outlawed, Du Bois insisted that equal rights for blacks were still missing from American society. A man of staggering intellect and drive, Du Bois was the first black to hold a doctorate from Harvard University and was one of the founders of the NAACP. He wrote three historical works, two novels, two autobiographies, and sixteen pioneering books on sociology, history, politics, and race relations, including the monumental achievement *The Souls of Black Folk*. Du Bois also shaped the concept of a black intellectual elite, or a "Talented Tenth" of politicians, writers, and thinkers who would unite black America and foster the idea of blacks as a race of forceful and creative thinkers.

In 1963 on the day of the civil rights march in Washington, a speaker arrived with the news that Du Bois had died that momentous day at the age of 95. A hush descended over the huge crowd. A pall had settled because the man most responsible for the event would not be able to see it. Such was the power of Du Bois's personality, drive, intellect, and vision.

Black Betty (1994)

Walter Mosley
Novel

B *lack Betty* is the fourth, and the strongest, installment in the Easy Rawlins mystery series. The time is the late 1940s, the place is Los Angeles, and the living is hard. Ezekial "Easy" Rawlins, a former soldier who is still hurting from the departure of his wife to Mississippi with another man, is facing pressure from his real estate dealings and from the challenges of raising two children. Desperate for work, he takes on an offer to find a woman, Elizabeth Eady, *a.k.a.* Black Betty, who has vanished into thin air. Her wealthy employer wants her back, and so the search begins. Add Mouse, Easy's sidekick, and murder and mayhem soon follow.

Mosley writes mystery, yes; but he also suffuses his stories with a deeply intimate knowledge of the black community and its struggles. This passage from *Black Betty* illustrates Mosley's skill at re-creating the surface and depth of life in the middle-class black communities of Los Angeles while at the same time addressing, in his two-fisted way, the existential issues that dog all African Americans:

> On the bus there were mainly old people and young mothers and teenagers coming in late to school. Most of them were black people. Dark-skinned with generous features. Women with eyes so deep that most men can never know them. Women like Betty who'd lost too much to be silly or kind. And there were the children, like Spider and Terry T once were, with futures so bleak it could make you cry just to hear them laugh. Because behind the music of their laughing you knew there was the rattle of chains. Chains we wore for no crime; chains we wore for so long that they melded with our bones. We all carry them

216

but nobody can see it—not even most of us. All the way home I thought about freedom coming for us at last. But what about all those centuries in chains? Where do they go when you get free?

All that and a mystery, too.

Mosley continues a tradition of African American detective fiction that uses this genre to explore issues of empowerment, a tradition begun by novelists like Chester Himes (*If He Hollers Let Him Go* and *A Rage in Harlem*), W. Adolphe Roberts (*The Haunting Hand*, 1926), and Rudolph Fisher (*The Conjure Man Dies*, 1932). Other books in the acclaimed Easy Rawlins series include *Gone Fishing, Devil in a Blue Dress, A Little Yellow Dog, A Red Death,* and *White Butterfly.*

Brotherman: The Odyssey of Black Men in America—An Anthology (1995)

Edited by Herb Boyd and Robert L. Allen
Anthology

"**B**rotherman" is a special greeting among black men. It is a verbal handshake, a shared mantra that expresses much more than a mere hello, that carries a number of meanings for black men no matter who they are. Their coded exchange of "brotherman" signals immediate recognition and rapport. It conveys a message that is at once an affirmation, an affectionate embrace, and a battle cry that proclaims "We have a common fate—what happens to one happens to all."

By creating "a living mosaic of essays and stories in which black men can view themselves, and be viewed without distortion," *Brotherman* opens a world that very few people get to see: "the world that the black man experiences as adolescents, lovers, husbands, fathers, workers, warriors, and elders."

Brotherman, the first collection of its kind, gives tribute to the resiliency of black men's creativity, intellect, and endurance by showcasing their greatest writers, public figures, and spokesmen: Howard Thurman, Amiri Baraka, Martin Luther King Jr., Nathan McCall, W. E. B. Du Bois, Malcolm X, Claude Brown, Alex Haley, Langston Hughes, James Baldwin, Marcus Garvey, Chester Himes, Ralph Ellison, John Edgar Wideman, Ishmael Reed, and many others.

Each piece is a unique experience because it presents a part of the puzzle that is the black man. Whether these parts add up to a whole is not the point; that the collection gives insight into the psyche of a lover, brother, friend, father, or neighbor is what secures its place in literary history.

Index of Books by Title

Africa Must Unite	113
Annie Allen	168
The Autobiography of Malcolm X	204
The Autobiography of Miss Jane Pittman	174
Before the Mayflower	30
Beloved	40
Black Betty	216
Black Bourgeoisie	107
Black Boy	66
The Blacker the Berry	61
The Black Jacobins	111
Black Macho and the Myth of the Superwoman	178
Black Metropolis: A Study of Negro Life in a Northern City	68
Black Power	116
Black Reconstruction in America	24
Black Skin, White Masks	82
A Black Theology of Liberation	143
Blues People: Negro Music in White America	78
Brotherman	218
Brothers and Keepers	207
Cane	58
The Chaneysville Incident	38
Clotel: or, the President's Daughter, A Narrative of Slave Life in the United States	17
The Color Purple	180
The Conjure Woman	55
Conversations with God: Two Centuries of Prayers by African Americans	151
The Crisis of the Negro Intellectual	84
Damballah	91

The Daughters of Africa	190
David Walker's Appeal	103
The Destruction of Black Civilization	123
Elbow Room	90
Faith and the Good Thing	146
The Famished Road	147
Fences	208
The Fire Next Time	109
for colored girls who have considered suicide/when the rainbow is enuf	176
From Slavery to Freedom: A History of African Americans	26
Go Tell It on the Mountain	72
God's Bits of Wood	131
Guide My Feet: Prayers and Meditation on Loving and Working for Children	153
A Hard Road to Glory: A History of the African American Athlete	93
The Hero and the Blues	87
I Know Why the Caged Bird Sings	171
If He Hollers Let Him Go	202
The Interesting Narrative of the Life of Olaudah Equiano, or Gustavus Vassa, the African, Written by Himself	13
Invisible Man	70
Jesus and the Disinherited	139
Jubilee	80
Kehinde	189
Kindred	43
Krik? Krak!	95
A Lesson Before Dying	214
Letter from a Birmingham Jail	141
The Life of Langston Hughes	210
Lyrics of Lowly Life	53
The Man Who Cried I Am	209
Manchild in the Promised Land	206
Maud Martha	170
Miles: The Autobiography	212

The Mis-education of the Negro	62
Mumbo Jumbo	145
My Soul Is a Witness: African American Women's Spirituality	155
The Narrative of the Life and Times of Frederick Douglass: An American Slave, Written by Himself	15
Native Son	201
The New Negro	59
Notes of a Hanging Judge	127
Our Nig, or Sketches from the Life of a Free Black, in a Two-Story White House, North	19
The Philosophy and Opinions of Marcus Garvey; or Africa for the Africans	105
Praisesong for the Widow	183
Race Matters	129
A Raisin in the Sun	76
The River Between	115
Roots: The Saga of an American Family	35
Sally Hemings	37
Seize the Time: The Story of the Black Panther Party	121
Sister Outsider: Essays and Speeches	185
Sojourner Truth: A Life, a Symbol	192
Soledad Brother: The Prison Letters of George Jackson	119
Song of Solomon	88
Soul on Ice	118
The Souls of Black Folk	56
Spirits of the Passage: The Transatlantic Slave Trade in the Seventeenth Century	45
The Spook Who Sat by the Door	125
Stolen Legacy	28
The Street	167
The Substance of Things Hoped For	157
Tapping the Power Within	149
Their Eyes Were Watching God	165
They Came Before Columbus	33
Things Fall Apart	74

Two Thousand Seasons	32
Up from Slavery	22
W. E. B. Du Bois: Biography of a Race	215
Waiting to Exhale	187
The Ways of White Folks	64
We a BaddDDD People	86
The Women of Brewster Place	179
The Wretched of the Earth	112
Your Blues Ain't Like Mine	188

Index of Books by Author

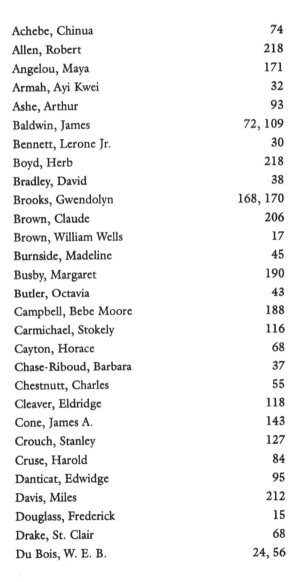

Achebe, Chinua	74
Allen, Robert	218
Angelou, Maya	171
Armah, Ayi Kwei	32
Ashe, Arthur	93
Baldwin, James	72, 109
Bennett, Lerone Jr.	30
Boyd, Herb	218
Bradley, David	38
Brooks, Gwendolyn	168, 170
Brown, Claude	206
Brown, William Wells	17
Burnside, Madeline	45
Busby, Margaret	190
Butler, Octavia	43
Campbell, Bebe Moore	188
Carmichael, Stokely	116
Cayton, Horace	68
Chase-Riboud, Barbara	37
Chestnutt, Charles	55
Cleaver, Eldridge	118
Cone, James A.	143
Crouch, Stanley	127
Cruse, Harold	84
Danticat, Edwidge	95
Davis, Miles	212
Douglass, Frederick	15
Drake, St. Clair	68
Du Bois, W. E. B.	24, 56

Dunbar, Paul Laurence	53
Edelman, Marian Wright	153
Ellison, Ralph	70
Emecheta, Buchi	189
Equiano, Olaudah	13
Fanon, Frantz	82, 112
Franklin, John Hope	26
Frazier, E. Franklin	107
Gaines, Ernest	174, 214
Garvey, Marcus	105
Greenlee, Sam	125
Haley, Alex	35, 204
Hamilton, Charles V.	116
Hansberry, Lorraine	76
Himes, Chester	202
Hughes, Langston	64
Hurston, Zora Neale	165
Jackson, George	119
James, C. L. R.	111
James, George G. M.	28
Johnson, Charles	146
Jones, LeRoi	78
King, Martin Luther Jr.	141
Lewis, David Levering	215
Locke, Alain	59
Lorde, Audre	185
Marshall, Paule	183
McMillan, Terry	187
McPherson, James Alan	90
Morrison, Toni	40, 88
Mosley, Walter	216
Murray, Albert	87
Naylor, Gloria	179
Nkrumah, Dr. Kwame	113
Okri, Ben	147

Ousmane, Sembene	131
Painter, Nell Irvin	192
Petry, Anne	167
Proctor, Samuel DeWitt	157
Rampersad, Arnold	210
Reed, Ishmael	145
Robotham, Rosemarie	45
Sanchez, Sonia	86
Seale, Bobby	121
Shange, Ntozake	176
Thiongo, Ngugi Wa	115
Thurman, Howard	139
Thurman, Wallace	61
Toomer, Jean	58
Troupe, Quincy	212
Van Sertima, Ivan	33
Vanzant, Iyanla	149
Wade-Gayles, Gloria	155
Walker, Alice	180
Walker, David	103
Walker, Margaret	80
Wallace, Michele	178
Washington, Booker T.	22
Washington, James Melvin	151
West, Cornel	129
Wideman, John Edgar	91, 207
Williams, Chancellor	123
Williams, John Alfred	209
Wilson, August	208
Wilson, Harriet E.	19
Woodson, Carter G.	62
Wright, Richard	66, 201

Index of Books by Genre

Anthology

Brotherman, edited by Herb Boyd and Robert Allen — 218

Conversations with God: Two Centuries of Prayers by African Americans, edited by James Melvin Washington — 151

The Daughters of Africa, edited by Margaret Busby — 190

My Soul Is a Witness: African American Women's Spirituality, edited by Gloria Wade-Gayles — 155

The New Negro, edited by Alain Locke — 59

Biography and Memoir

The Autobiography of Malcolm X, as told to Alex Haley — 204

Black Boy, by Richard Wright — 66

Brothers and Keepers, by John Edgar Wideman — 207

I Know Why the Caged Bird Sings, by Maya Angelou — 171

The Interesting Narrative of the Life of Olaudah Equiano, or Gustavus Vassa, the African, Written by Himself, by Olaudah Equiano — 13

Letter from a Birmingham Jail, by Martin Luther King Jr. — 141

The Life of Langston Hughes, by Arnold Rampersad — 210

Manchild in the Promised Land, by Claude Brown — 206

Miles: The Autobiography, by Miles Davis (with Quincy Troupe) — 212

The Narrative of the Life and Times of Frederick Douglass: An American Slave, Written by Himself, by Frederick Douglass — 15

Sojourner Truth, by Nell Irvin Painter — 192

Soledad Brother: The Prison Letters of George Jackson, by George Jackson — 119

Soul on Ice, by Eldridge Cleaver — 118

The Substance of Things Hoped For, by Samuel DeWitt Proctor — 157

Up from Slavery, by Booker T. Washington — 22

W. E. B. Du Bois: Biography of a Race, by David Levering Lewis — 215

Drama

Fences, by August Wilson 208

for colored girls who have considered suicide/when the rainbow is enuf, by Ntozake Shange 176

A Raisin in the Sun, by Lorraine Hansberry 76

History

Before the Mayflower, by Lerone Bennett Jr. 30

Black Reconstruction in America, by W. E. B. Du Bois 24

The Black Jacobins, by C. L. R. James 111

The Destruction of Black Civilization, by Chancellor Williams 123

From Slavery to Freedom: A History of African Americans, by John Hope Franklin 26

A Hard Road to Glory: A History of the African American Athlete, by Arthur Ashe 93

Spirits of the Passage: The Transatlantic Slave Trade in the Seventeenth Century, by Madeline Burnside and Rosemarie Robotham 45

Stolen Legacy, by George G. M. James 28

They Came Before Columbus, by Ivan Van Sertima 33

Nonfiction

Africa Must Unite, by Kwame Nkrumah 113

Black Bourgeoisie, by E. Franklin Frazier 107

Black Macho and the Myth of the Superwoman, by Michele Wallace 178

Black Metropolis: A Study of Negro Life in a Northern City, by St. Clair Drake and Horace Cayton 68

Black Power, by Stokely Carmichael and Charles V. Hamilton 116

Black Skin, White Masks, by Frantz Fanon 82

A Black Theology of Liberation, by James A. Cone 143

Blues People: Negro Music in White America, by LeRoi Jones 78

The Crisis of the Negro Intellectual, by Harold Cruse 84

David Walker's Appeal, by David Walker 103

The Fire Next Time, by James Baldwin 109

Guide My Feet: Prayers and Meditation on Loving and Working for Children, by Marian Wright Edelman   153

The Hero and the Blues, by Albert Murray   87

Jesus and the Disinherited, by Howard Thurman   139

Letter from a Birmingham Jail, by Martin Luther King Jr.   141

The Mis-education of the Negro, by Carter G. Woodson   62

Notes of a Hanging Judge, by Stanley Crouch   127

The Philosophy and Opinions of Marcus Garvey; or Africa for the Africans, by Marcus Garvey   105

Race Matters, by Cornel West   129

Seize the Time: The Story of the Black Panther Party, by Bobby Seale   121

Sister Outsider: Essays and Speeches, by Audre Lorde   185

The Souls of Black Folk, by W. E. B. Du Bois   56

Tapping the Power Within, by Iyanla Vanzant   149

The Wretched of the Earth, by Frantz Fanon   112

Novels and Short Stories

The Autobiography of Miss Jane Pittman, by Ernest Gaines   174

Beloved, by Toni Morrison   40

Black Betty, by Walter Mosley   216

The Blacker the Berry, by Wallace Thurman   61

Cane, by Jean Toomer   58

The Chaneysville Incident, by David Bradley   38

Clotel: or, the President's Daughter, A Narrative of Slave Life in the United States, by William Wells Brown   17

The Color Purple, by Alice Walker   180

The Conjure Woman, by Charles Chestnutt   55

Damballah, by John Edgar Wideman   91

Elbow Room, by James Alan McPherson   90

Faith and the Good Thing, by Charles Johnson   146

The Famished Road, by Ben Okri   147

Go Tell It on the Mountain, by James Baldwin   72

God's Bits of Wood, by Sembene Ousmane   131

If He Hollers Let Him Go, by Chester Himes   202

Invisible Man, by Ralph Ellison 70

Jubilee, by Margaret Walker 80

Kehinde, by Buchi Emecheta 189

Kindred, by Octavia Butler 43

Krik? Krak!, by Edwidge Danticat 95

A Lesson Before Dying, by Ernest Gaines 214

The Man Who Cried I Am, by John A. Williams 209

Maud Martha, by Gwendolyn Brooks 170

Mumbo Jumbo, by Ishmael Reed 145

Native Son, by Richard Wright 201

Our Nig, or Sketches from the Life of a Free Black, in a Two-Story White House, North, by Harriet E. Wilson 19

Praisesong for the Widow, by Paule Marshall 183

The River Between, by Ngugi Wa Thiongo 115

Roots: The Saga of an American Family, by Alex Haley 35

Sally Hemings, by Barbara Chase-Riboud 37

Song of Solomon, by Toni Morrison 88

The Spook Who Sat by the Door, by Sam Greenlee 125

The Street, by Ann Petry 167

Their Eyes Were Watching God, by Zora Neale Hurston 165

Things Fall Apart, by Chinua Achebe 74

Two Thousand Seasons, by Ayi Kwei Armah 32

Waiting to Exhale, by Terry McMillan 187

The Ways of White Folks, by Langston Hughes 64

The Women of Brewster Place, by Gloria Naylor 179

Your Blues Ain't Like Mine, by Bebe Moore Campbell 188

Poetry

Annie Allen, by Gwendolyn Brooks 168

Lyrics of Lowly Life, by Paul Laurence Dunbar 53

We a BaddDDD People, by Sonia Sanchez 86

My Essential Books

Create your own list of essential books and forward them to QBR/ Sacred Fire, 625 Broadway, New York, NY 10012. We will publish them in QBR or post them on our web site (www.qbr.com). You may e-mail your list to: editor@qbr.com. Please include your name and address, including zip code.

Printed in the USA
CPSIA information can be obtained
at www.ICGtesting.com
JSHW082158140824
68134JS00014B/309